ACTIVE CITIZENS

Nick Fielding has worked for Shelter and NCVO, where he edited the weekly voluntary sector supplement to *New Society*. He was also Society editor for *New Statesman and Society*. He is now a freelance journalist and writer specialising in social policy issues, and contributes regular features to *The Independent* and *New Statesman and Society*, as well as writing for other newspapers and magazines. He is the author of *The Good Federation Guide*, and *Meeting the Need: Planning Alcohol Services for the 1990s*, and recently helped to write a major report on employment for the European Commission.

Gillian Reeve was educated at London University, and for most of her working life has combined freelance writing and editing with work as press and publications officer for a variety of voluntary organisations, most recently the Medical Campaign Against Nuclear Weapons. She has had two plays on BBC radio, is co-author (with Joan Smith) of *Offence of the Realm: How Peace Campaigners Get Bugged*, and has contributed articles and reviews to many journals and newspapers.

Margaret Simey was born in 1906 and has lived and worked in Liverpool for most of her adult life, where she served for over twenty years as a councillor and was chairwoman of the Merseyside Police Authority from 1981 to 1986. In 1988, Liverpool University awarded her an honorary doctorate in recognition of her service to the community, and made her a Senior Fellow (Hon) of the Department of Continuing Education. She is the author of several books, including *Government by Consent: the Principle of Accountability in Local Government*, also published by Bedford Square Press. As a member of Liverpool Housing Trust, she is currently campaigning to defend the voluntary status of the housing association movement.

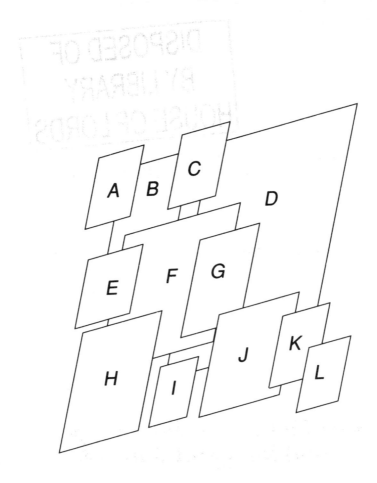

The portraits on the front cover are of some of the people whose stories appear in *Active Citizens*. Grateful thanks is given to all those interviewed for their time and co-operation.

A	Gordon Baxendale	G	Margaret Simey
B	Lalita Ahmed	H	David Wragg
C	Colin Low	I	Kath Cripps
D	David Bryan	J	Femi Otitoju
E	Jane Saxby	K	Christine Cardwell
F	Eleanor Holmes	L	Margy Woodward

The photograph of Jane Saxby is by John McDonald and that of David Bryan by Sharron Wallace. The photograph of Kath Cripps is reproduced by permission of Sheffield Newspapers Ltd.

ACTIVE CITIZENS

New Voices and Values

**Nick Fielding, Gillian Reeve
and Margaret Simey**

Bedford Square Press

Published by
BEDFORD SQUARE PRESS of the
National Council for Voluntary Organisations
26 Bedford Square, London WC1B 3HU

First published 1991
© Bedford Square Press, 1991

Typeset by AKM Associates (UK) Ltd, Southall, London
Printed and bound in Great Britain by Billings, Worcester
Cover printed by Heyford Press, Wellingborough

British Library Cataloguing in Publication Data
Fielding, Nick
    Active citizens: new voices and values. — (Society today).
    1. Great Britain.   Voluntary organisations
    I. Title   II. Reeve, Gillian   III. Simey, Margaret   IV. Series
    062

ISBN 0-7199-1273-3

Contents

Chapters 1, 14 and 15 were written by Margaret Simey, chapters 2, 3, 7, 8, 9 and 13 by Nick Fielding, and chapters 4, 5, 6, 10, 11 and 12 by Gillian Reeve.

Preface

Farewell the Voluntary Worker! Hail the Active Citizen! True or false? Is this book by way of being a wake for a dying tradition, or does it celebrate the birth of a new vision which will carry us bravely forward into the unknown world of the next century?

Our aim is to introduce some plain thinking into the rhetoric of public pronouncements about active citizenship which confuse and befuddle us and divert the voluntary movement from its true intention. The politicians have stolen our clothes and we shiver with apprehension and resentment. The government's promotion of active citizenship – most recently expressed in the report of the Speaker's Commission on Citizenship published in September 1990 – has seemed to concentrate on urging people to share their time or wealth with, or care for, those less fortunate than themselves and on encouraging them to take more responsibility for the creation of a civil, safe and tidy environment. Those of us reared in the tradition of voluntary service find it totally unacceptable that volunteering should thus be reduced to the status of an optional extra for the virtuous citizen, something that is no more than a patronising expression of compassion for those less successful than we are ourselves.

No one would deny the importance of the need for us to take our civic responsibilities more seriously. There are many voluntary organisations which tend to reflect this point of view, such as the WRVS and environmental groups working for a tidier Britain, and this strand is duly represented among the active citizens portrayed here. Many in the voluntary sector, however, are seriously concerned that this emphasis leaves out other long-standing and equally important elements in the voluntary work movement. For example, it omits all reference to the dogged campaign to give people the right and opportunity to voice their own needs rather than being merely cared for. It also fails to take account of the century-long struggle to extend to all and sundry some share in the responsibility for the common good. Indeed, the more activist type of worker in general seems to be in danger of being left out of the government's picture of the active citizen. This book therefore also gives voice to this extremely important element of voluntary work.

How has it come about that voluntary work should so have diminished in stature that it can be defined negatively as being merely 'non-governmental'? To understand the current situation it is essential to set it in the framework of the past. Only if we understand how we come to be where we are now can we hope to make our way into the uncertain future which lies before us. Part 1 accordingly tells the story of the far-reaching changes that have taken place in the relationship between voluntary work and the state following on the creation of the welfare state and its assumption of many of the responsibilities previously left to the individual conscience. It is a story characterised by the dogged insistence of an increasingly wide variety of individuals, on their right to make a personal contribution to the well being of the community to which they belong.

The second part of the book then addresses the present: what of volunteering today? Nick Fielding and Gillian Reeve tell the stories, through interviews, of a group of 'active citizens' who are involved in women's issues, tenants' organisations, the peace movement, environmental action, black issues and other areas of work throughout the UK. The profile with which this section concludes attempts to define what sort of people these are who spontaneously devote so much of their time and energy, often for little tangible reward, in order to right some wrong, remedy some deficiency, or just to love their neighbours. All this makes clear the urgency of the need to re-think the traditional definition of 'voluntary' in order to accommodate the extensive changes which have taken place over the past century in the nature of voluntary work and of those who undertake it. The stereotype no longer fits the reality.

What then of the future? It is with this that Part 3 is concerned. Clearly, there can be no standing still, no opting out in a world where the very way of life which gave rise to the voluntary movement as such is itself under threat. There can be no evasion of the question as to whether there will any longer be room for the likes of 'Us', the volunteers, in a world increasingly dominated by 'Them', those in authority to whom we so frequently delegate our social responsibilities. The answer must be a confident re-affirmation of the basic principles of the right of the individual to social responsibility together with a searching examination of how best this can be effectively exercised in the contemporary world. We hope that, by stimulating discussion of issues of such fundamental importance, a positive and creative response can be made to the challenge of the active citizen.

Bedford Square Press joins us in thanking the Calouste Gulbenkian Foundation for their generous financial assistance in meeting the costs of writing and producing this book.

Nick Fielding
Gillian Reeve
Margaret Simey

PART ONE

THE PAST

Margaret Simey

CHAPTER 1

REFLECTIONS OF A VOLUNTARY WORKER

As a volunteer, I have been a thorn in the flesh, a critic on the hearth of officialdom, a dissenter who refused to accept the weary world as it is.

If I tell the story of volunteering in the past largely in terms of what happened in Liverpool, it is not only because it is the city I know best but also because of the leading part its citizens have always played in current developments in voluntary work. And if I present it largely in terms of my own experience that is because all my life I have been a voluntary worker and have myself lived through, at first hand, the astonishing changes which voluntary work has undergone in the course of my life-time.

Apart from a few years as a youth leader before I married, I have always been a 'kept wife', doing whatever I did from choice and not for money. That was the way of the world in which I grew up. As a volunteer, I have been a thorn in the flesh, a critic on the hearth of officialdom, a dissenter who refused to accept this weary world as it is. And in so doing, I have trodden the very same path as the band of voluntary workers whose words are recorded in the second part of this book. It is in the light of that common experience that it falls to me to attempt to extract the thread of the long story of those who throughout the century have maintained the proud tradition of voluntary work in this country.

In the Beginning: Method versus Muddle

The story starts neatly enough with the beginning of the century. The issue of the day was the continued existence of extreme poverty in the midst of dazzling wealth – a problem which baffled economists and social reformers alike, as indeed it does to this day. A Royal Commission was set up in 1905 to examine the existing means of relieving poverty and to suggest changes. Endless arguments ensued, provoked not least by Beatrice Webb, herself a member of the Commission and a voluntary worker if ever there was one. The Commission accumulated masses of evidence and produced a mammoth Report in 1909 but, at the end of the day, their recommendations focused mainly on the detail of the reform of the Poor Law. It was only when Beatrice set out on a great campaign to promote her own particular proposals that she realised that the Report had left high and dry the question of the effect of its proposals on the relationship between the state and the volunteer. To her astonishment, this was evidently a matter of great interest to her audiences, and she promptly adapted her speeches to include it.

True to its philanthropic tradition, Liverpool was one of the first of the big cities to tackle the implications of the proposed changes. The woolly recommendation of the 1909 Report that it would be a good idea to set up co-ordinating councils of voluntary service in every town was promptly followed by the formation of the Liverpool Council of Voluntary Aid. This was designed to introduce method into the chaotic muddle of the voluntary effort in the city. Working parties were set up to bring together the disheartened and bewildered charitable agencies as a first step towards co-ordinating the medley of effort. Chaired by leading businessmen, good progress was made on all fronts.

The Social Improvement and Education working party concerned itself with the social disintegration and lack of administrative structure which characterised the situation in Liverpool, as in every big city. It brought together an unprecedented variety of talent. There were academics from the young University of Liverpool, who had chosen to abandon the traditional fields of the old universities in favour of the industrial north. There were merchants, mainly Nonconformists, who stood for the philanthropic tradition for which the city was already famous. And there were local women who were deeply involved in the lively campaign for the emancipation of their sex. Together they came up with a quite remarkable blue-print designed to promote the vision of the Urban City as the finest flower of the Industrial Revolution. Considering the image of the industrial towns, as 'dark satanic mills', this was indeed an astonishing proposition. All the more so because of the basic principle upon which the whole concept depended. This was no less than the working party's unshakeable conviction that the right to a share in the responsibility for the general welfare was an attribute of citizenship which must be universally enjoyed. Every man Jack – and every woman Jill – must be entitled to exercise this responsibility as of right, however humble or illiterate he or she might be.

Not content with fine phrases, this little band set to work to prepare and implement proposals for putting their principle into practice. How they set about this forbidding task and what fortunes befell them makes a splendid story from which we today have much to learn. Who knows what might have come of their work had the outbreak of war in 1914 not disrupted their plans and brought changes which entirely altered the situation which they had been designed to meet.

Aftermath of the 1914–18 War

Everybody was taken by surprise by the sudden huge increase in the demands for the relief of families following the call-up of so many of the bread-winners. No machinery existed which could cope with such a situation, apart from a fading organisation set up to deal with the relief of soldiers' and sailors' families during the Boer War. Sympathy ran away with sense and what had been a chaotic situation before became much worse. In despair, the Lord Mayor turned to his cousin, Eleanor Rathbone, who had for some years been training women for voluntary work under the auspices of the Victoria Settlement. Mary Stocks describes in her biography of Eleanor (*Eleanor Rathbone*, 1949) the astonishing speed and efficiency with which these cohorts of women rose to an opportunity such as they had never dreamed of. By the end of the war, two lessons had been learned. Firstly, a great increase in state intervention had to be accepted. Secondly, women, especially from the middle classes, must be allowed to play a far larger part in the world at large than ever before.

But what of voluntary work? Where did the social conscience of the individual come in? Burdened though they were, Eleanor and her colleagues on the working party (one of whom was Fred Marquis, the future Lord Woolton who was destined to become the major domo of the Ministry of Food in the Second World War) never gave up their search for an answer. Many of the dreamers had been killed in the war, but the dream lived on. An increase in state benefits would have to be accepted, but they were wholly convinced that material relief was not the whole story. The more benefits the state provided for people's needs, the more complicated the machinery required for their administration. Such public assistance as was available was hedged about with a labyrinth of rules and regulations which defeated many of those who applied. 'The poor' needed someone to be on their side, to advise them in their dealings with those in authority and, more subtly but none the less importantly, to care about their distress. Moreover, it was in meeting that need and maintaining a personal relationship between the community and those in need that all those who hungered to give service to others and to be of value to society would themselves find fulfilment.

The outcome was the setting up of a Personal Service Society (PSS), effectively a splinter group of members of the LCVA who banded together to defend the principle and practice of personal voluntary service. Their purpose was to provide the machinery whereby each and every citizen could voluntarily give and receive service, according to their capacity and their need. Out of that modest attempt to provide a counter-weight to what was one day to become the welfare state developed the nationwide service provided today by the citizens advice bureaux.

The instant demand which deluged the little agency brought major difficulties. When Dorothy Keeling, who was appointed as organiser, wrote her autobiography, she called it *The Crowded Stair* because of the queues of applicants who chronically blocked the passage up to her office. The sheer bulk of poverty had always been a particular problem in Liverpool, but the aftermath of the First World War multiplied it to unmanageable proportions. The agency had to face the fact that volunteers simply could not deal with such a volume of demand and that a nucleus of paid staff would have to be employed. Moreover, the complexity of the problems brought by the clients demanded a response that was plainly beyond the capacity or the good-will of the average volunteer. Every worker would have to be trained and supervised. Casework, as it came to be called, could no longer be a matter for spontaneous charity; it must become a recognised profession.

Nevertheless, Dorothy remained adamant that there was all the difference in the world between working for a voluntary body and being employed by the state, even if the 'volunteer' was in fact a paid professional. How we used to wrangle over the apparent contradiction of that distinction. There were even those who argued that it was impossible to be both a civil servant and a committed Christian because loyalty to the state would over-rule the freedom of the individual conscience. Rather the paltry pay of the 'voluntary' social worker than the comparatively lush pastures of the 'slavery' of the civil service. Those were the days when we wore our social worker hats as a badge of honour.

Eleanor Rathbone and her colleagues, who fought so hard for education and opportunities for women, can have had no idea of the far-reaching consequences of that apparently minor decision by a small voluntary society to pay women to do what they had previously done voluntarily, and to train them for it. As it turned out, opportunities for employment such as were offered by agencies like the PSS came as a heaven-sent chance for the regiment of 'superfluous women' left high and dry after the First World War ended. Their wartime service had enabled women to escape from domesticity. They had tasted independence. They had undertaken all kinds of jobs and knew that they could do them. But once the war had ended, they found themselves unwanted. There was no room for them. Men back from the forces inevitably claimed priority for such work as was available; the Great Depression was already casting its dark gloom over the economic scene. At the same time, there was no hope of retreating into marriage because of the slaughter of young men in the war. The option of staying at home as an unmarried daughter was no longer available in the changed economic climate. It is hard to convey to the 1990s the extraordinary surrealism of that world of unwanted women. I was a cadet in the suffrage movement at that time and recollect student dances at which there might well be not a solitary man with whom to dance.

It was that experience of frustration and rejection which fired our enthusiasm for the movement for the emancipation of women. I myself was so caught up in the fun and companionship of the campaign to secure the election of Eleanor Rathbone as Independent Member of Parliament for the Combined Universities (a seat now abolished) that I nearly failed my degree. We fought for the Vote because it stood as the symbol of our right to be active citizens in the most literal sense of the word. Our ambition was something totally different from our traditional role as do-ers of good which we had carried out for generations; we were simply not interested in voluntary work. When the principle of equal citizenship was won, it was therefore galling in the extreme to be denied the opportunity to take our place in the world at large. Imagine, then, the attraction of the prospect of employment as a paid social worker in an occupation where men were not in competition!

Enter the New Philanthropist

Though I was blissfully unaware of the fact, I was myself typecast as one of these 'New Philanthropists'. I had been reared in the tradition of the unpaid voluntary worker, my mother being an active member of the church women's section and I myself a Sunday School teacher. What more natural than that when I went to University, the first woman in the family to do so, I should be attracted by the prospect of earning my living as a social worker. I was fortunate in that, at that very moment, thought was being given to setting up a memorial to the great Charles Booth, which was to provide the very opportunity I was seeking.

Charles Booth was a member of one of the leading merchant families in Liverpool, a shipowner whose Booth Line had pioneered one of the first tourist cruises, the Thousand-Miles-Up-The-Amazon trip. He was also the author of the massive survey of the *Life and Labour of the People of London* which appeared in instalments between 1886 and 1902. His survey was planned as a scientific corrective to what were regarded as hysterical claims that poverty existed on a vast scale. To Booth's surprise, it demonstrated a widespread deprivation far worse than he had expected. This huge enterprise was an outstanding piece of voluntary work involving vast expenditure of his own time and money.

The memorial to Booth took the form of a Charles Booth Chair of Social Science at the University of Liverpool, (a post which, incidentally, my husband was one day to occupy). This was designed primarily to promote the study of a novel subject – society. I had gone to the University of Liverpool with a vague notion that I might become a teacher of geography, but I instantly abandoned the idea and enrolled as a student on the new course, the first ever, so I was told, to take a degree in this hitherto unheard-of subject. Practical training for social workers was also provided, though reluctantly as it was not considered to be academically respectable. Most of the people undertaking this training were voluntary workers, such as the wives of clergy or workers in various charities. All bar two were women.

Little did I foresee what a threat I and others like me were to become to the established order. I blush to remember with what condescension we regarded volunteers. We were professionals. We knew. Volunteers were of a lesser species, only to be tolerated as handmaidens, hopefully to be phased out as amateur dabblers who might well do more harm than good. Inevitably, the paid workers rose to the top, meekly though they might address the members of their Committees. The high-handed way Dorothy Keeling treated her voluntary chauffeur, the daughter of an important local family, became part of the folklore of students in training. As in the PSS so elsewhere, women flooded into this new and expanding job market. As fast as a new social need was uncovered, and a new specialism was devised to meet it, women swept in and took over. It could almost be said that women invented social work as a career in order to meet their own desperate need. There was little room here for amateurs.

It had been expected of me as a degree student that I would pioneer the entry of women into the expanding civil service brought into being by the increase in state welfare provision. What was, at the time, a high ambition held little attraction for me. I was even less tempted by the prospect of a career as a case worker: the closed-shop attitude of the professionals who dealt with the relief of the miseries of the poor repelled me. I was an out-going type, an enthusiastic folk-dancer who was essentially sociable. I had myself belonged to a curious little girls' club attached to a church, called the Camp Fire Girls. Without hesitation, I headed for what was called group work.

Voluntary Service and the Community

At that stage, I certainly failed to realise the significance of the fact that the girls' club movement depended almost entirely on voluntary effort, although it had begun to attract a certain degree of official approval as a response to the 'youth problem' of the war years. The leading figure in youth work in Liverpool at that time was an ex-social science student called Josephine Duckworth. Joey Duck, as she was invariably called, was herself employed as the organiser of the Liverpool Union of Girls' Clubs but, at heart, she was an instinctive volunteer. A committed Christian, she felt that a voluntary worker was someone who gave absolute priority to that inner light called conscience. Certainly, the state should provide resources for youth work but there was no way she would permit any sort of official interference in the independence of a club and its members. It was no business of the state if a girls' club decided to conclude its evening programme with prayer or by standing on its head: the members must be free to make their own decisions. At a time when grants in aid of youth work were hard to come by, it was a brave stand to take. The vigour with which Joey and her regiment of voluntary workers defended their position was a constant source of inspiration – and entertainment – to us all.

It was on the back of the youth movement that voluntary work by local people for the benefit of the community as a whole began to develop. In particular, those men and women returning from the forces to the new housing estates found much to be desired in the land fit for heroes which they had been promised. These were people with no experience of voluntary work in the middle-class tradition of charitable effort, but quite spontaneously they began to come together in little local groups to struggle to improve conditions. Unhappily, the pressure of problems on the big new estates deflected the energies of such groups into arguments with their landlord, the corporation or 'corpy', and this earned the community movement, as a whole, opposition from councillors and officials alike. It was thanks to sturdy work by people like Jane Saxby, whose story is told on pages 19–24, that community centres and councils survived.

To be fair, the official lack of appreciation has to be seen in the context of the Great Depression of the 1930s. Houses and jobs were not just a top priority; they were the only things that mattered. Demands for social facilities such as community centres or shops, or even churches, simply could not compete with that fearful urgency. Only public houses were available on the new estates and, in those days, women were not welcome in them. As official schemes for tackling the continuing distress multiplied, the drift to central control over their administration increased. There was little scope in those days of universal stress for the amateur endeavours of voluntary citizens, however active.

It was a drift which received a fresh impetus as a result of the evacuation of children from the inner cities on the outbreak of the Second World War in 1939. People living in the suburbs and affluent country dwellers were scandalised by the way of life of 'the poor' who invaded their orderly homes. The evacuees for their part, as in the case of the little family who arrived on my own doorstep, were equally dismayed by the lack of warmth or communal feeling in the welcome they received from the local community and quickly returned to wherever they had come from. I doubt if any increase of compassion or mutual understanding resulted from that entire exercise, but there was at least a fixed determination that 'something must be done' to improve conditions in the inner cities. So urgent was the need for action seen to be, that the Beveridge Plan for the setting up of the welfare state was actually published before the end of the war, in 1943. From then on, every energy was devoted to the preparation of the intricate legislation required to implement Beveridge's proposals and the setting up of the machinery necessary for their administration. Once again, as so often before, voluntary workers were left standing on the side-lines, bewildered and uncertain as to what to do next.

Voluntary Workers and the Welfare State

Surely, there would be no need for charity in the wonderful world of the welfare state? What was there left for middle-class, well-meaning do-gooders to do? I was Chairman of the Victoria Settlement in Scotland Road at the time, and I still remember how we agonised as to what our role should be in this new world, if indeed we had one. Fortunately, the local residents had no such doubts. For all its deprivations, they hankered after the way of life as it used to be in the 'Scotty Road' days of old and they were determined to restore it. The traditional Settlement committee was reconstituted as a community council of local representatives and was duly launched in 1947 by the Lord and Lady Mayoress, accompanied by the footmen and potted palms which always graced their public appearances. A large measure of responsibility for the management of the Settlement's affairs was thereby handed over to local volunteers. The input by daughters of the suburbs diminished accordingly.

This struggling new development was reflected elsewhere in the city. However, it only made progress after it received an unexpected boost as a consequence of the realisation by planners, in particular, that people must themselves be involved in the huge programme for the regeneration of the decaying industrial towns. Participation became the catch-phrase of the day and the community centres found themselves the subject of a degree of interest and approval such as had never before come their way. As the stringencies of the postwar period came to an end, resources became more readily available so that the swinging sixties brought a new optimism to all manner of little voluntary groups. Great numbers of people found opportunities for voluntary activity in connection with clearance schemes. The old tradition of voluntary work as essentially middle-class gave way to a dawning grasp of the fact that every citizen who wanted to contribute to the general well-being was entitled to do so, and should be given every encouragement.

Peter Walker, for example, then Minister for the Environment, actually presented a report to an international conference of Habitat in Sweden under the revealing title of *50 Million Volunteers* (1969).

This was based on the assumption that the nature of voluntary work was changing. It was no longer confined to a minority, but must be regarded as the natural means by which individuals were involved in the life of the community. Every voluntary activity – be it a pop group, an old people's dinner club, or a football team – constituted an act of citizenship and deserved to be fostered as such.

Understandably, in the general enthusiasm few reflected on the likely outcome that partnership surely implied a new contract between the 'partners'. As members of the community councils developed confidence and know-how, they began to look for increased responsibility in actually making the decisions and even spending the money – public money, no less. There was even talk of their becoming cogs in the machinery of local government as a species of urban parish councils. Fuel was added to these growing demands by the lack of co-ordination on the part of the public services. Each ministry devised its own programme in isolation and I remember how skilled the voluntary bodies became at playing the fruit machine of the grants system.

Eventually, in 1969, the government set up Community Development Projects in a number of cities to try out the practicalities of devolving responsibility right down to the grass roots at the point at which services were actually delivered. However, to the dismay of those in authority, all of the projects came up with the same unwelcome conclusion that nothing short of a drastic overhaul of the entire system of administration would serve to remedy the situation – a conclusion with which many local voluntary groups heartily agreed.

Alarmed to find their authority challenged by what was interpreted as Marxism and increasingly absorbed in the problems of the inner cities, official support for community development rapidly evaporated throughout the seventies. Talk of democracy was all very fine, but the people were not ready for it yet, we were told. How often I had heard that story in the West Indies before they won their independence! Faced with the inadequacies of local government, then the subject of government inquiry, more and more control was shifted to the centre. The dream of government by universal consent was replaced by the reality of government by remote control, in the last resort to be imposed by the police as the riots of 1981 bore witness. The gulf between Them and Us became a fact of life. Sadly, much of the interest in voluntary service which had been generated by the community movement in the 1960s simply faded away. The subsequent decade of Thatcherism has brought about changes so far-reaching as to suggest that it is unlikely that the ebbing tide of enthusiasm for voluntary service will easily be reversed, certainly not in its traditional form.

The Continuing Tradition of Voluntary Service

This is the situation we face today. It would be easy to end my reflections on a note of uncertainty and despondency. The long argument which has dominated my brief history of voluntary work in this century has been all about the relationship between government and governed, and their respective roles and responsibilities. 'They' appear to have won so much of the territory that all that is left for 'Us' would seem to be to resign ourselves to minding our personal affairs and enjoying as much of the undoubted pleasures of affluence as may come our way. Voluntaryism would seem to be on the way out.

And yet . . . and yet . . . The whole burden of my story is to the contrary. Right down the years there have always been some who have refused to be denied their right to care for others and who have insisted on loving their neighbour according to some private vision of their own. This gallant band have had to shift their ground constantly as the state has advanced deep into territory which was once regarded as sacrosanct to the individual conscience, but the determined refusal to accept their exclusion from social responsibility has never been quenched. Like a peat fire, it has gone underground only to break through the surface in unexpected bursts of flame.

What is this elusive 'voluntary' quality that all the argument has been, and still is, about? How can the advancing power of the professional bureaucracy, whether it is employed by statutory or voluntary agencies, be brought to acknowledge the vital importance of the principle that the responsibility for caring about our fellow human beings must be shared with each and every one of us? The answers must come from the many who, largely unseen and unsung, to this day carry on the tradition of voluntary service. Of these, the handful whose experiences are described in the second part of this book give some idea of the rich diversity of active citizens today.

PART TWO

THE PRESENT

Nick Fielding, Gillian Reeve
and Margaret Simey

PART 2

The backgrounds of the volunteers whose portraits appear in the following pages are as different as any dozen or so people picked out of a crowd at random. And yet, despite these different starting points, it is remarkable just how much this small group of people has in common.

Nick Fielding and Gillian Reeve took a conscious decision to include within this group people who reflected to some degree the prevailing trends within volunteering. Hence they have included eight women and four men. Figures produced by the Charities Aid Foundation and others have shown consistently that women volunteer more than men. The 1988/89 Charity Household Survey showed that more women gave time to volunteering than men, and that women who did volunteer did so for more hours than men. There is also a bias towards including people at both the older and younger ages of the spectrum. Generally (and for obvious reasons), the 24–40 age group is the least involved in voluntary activity. Health and welfare issues figure strongly in the activities of our group and, again, the Charities Aid Foundation figures show that these are two of the most prominent areas for which people volunteer.

The selection of people for interview has paid no heed to the definition of voluntary work as being an activity undertaken without financial reward, for the benefit of others. In its place, as a rule of thumb, the much more comprehensive notion of 'volunteering' has been adopted which sees it as an activity taking place outside the state, that is, it is 'non-governmental'. It is, however, the use of 'non-governmental' in this context which gives rise to the confusion in people's minds as to the distinction between active citizenship and voluntary service. This important issue will be discussed in the last two chapters of the book.

The portraits begin with the remarkable story of Jane Saxby, with half a lifetime of voluntary experience behind her, and still a very active citizen. She is followed by three people from ethnic minority backgrounds. Both Lalita Ahmed and David Bryan have worked principally with people from their own communities, supporting them in their struggles for better access to social and democratic rights. Femi Otitoju has taken this further to challenge the racial, sexual and gender stereotypes which exist within society.

Christine Cardwell, through her work for Women's Aid, has also chosen to work around issues which have directly affected her as a woman. She is one of seven people who work for a voluntary organisation in this sample. Like most of them, her voluntary activities are not confined to her job.

Eleanor Holmes, who is a full-time unpaid organiser for the Women's Royal Voluntary Service (WRVS) and a thoroughly professional volunteer, is one of the many thousands of people who make enormous personal sacrifices through their voluntary activity.

People with disabilities often tend to be thought of as the recipients of help from voluntary organisations. But both Colin Low, who is blind, and Margy Woodward, who has cerebral palsy, show that their disabilities are no hindrance to becoming actively involved in social issues. Their contributions are particularly important in an era when empowerment of disabled people is a growing issue.

The last four studies are of people whose voluntary activities are amongst the most widespread in the voluntary sector. David Wragg is a committed environmentalist. Kath Cripps stood up for her belief in a non-nuclear future and lost her position as a magistrate. Gordon Baxendale and Iris Williams are tenant activists, typical of many thousands of others throughout the country, while Elaine Appelbee's Christian belief is the inspiration for her work on an inner-city estate in Bradford.

In the final chapter to part 2, Margaret Simey then looks at what this group of individuals have in common to draw a profile of a voluntary worker.

CHAPTER 2

JANE SAXBY

I quite expect the time will come when I have to say 'no', but it's not yet. Because I get a lot out of doing it – enormous satisfaction and self-esteem.

Jane Saxby is a phenomenon. At the age of 85 she still goes old-time dancing twice a week and spends much of her time speaking to groups of old people, and to social workers and other professionals about the problems of old age. Her diary is booked up for months in advance.

She is an engaging conversationalist with a remarkable eye for detail and a directness which is refreshing. Her life story is one of almost constant involvement with communities and people around her in her native Liverpool.

What marks Jane out perhaps more than anything else from many people of her generation is her willingness to speak about the issue of sexuality amongst the old.

My husband and I were very happy. We had a sexual marriage for 50-odd years which I think, at the time, was unusual. I think it's quite important to stress this in later life because in many marriages in those days, women – both sexes in fact – were ignorant, and the actual situation leading up to a marriage night could be an appalling one with no one telling you what to expect, and a man with urgent needs and desires having held himself in for a long time could become a bit of a monster. I've had people tell me about this experience that marriage could be rape. It could have a life-long effect on the woman. I think this affected most women of my generation.

Jane now spends part of her time talking to social workers about the denial by professionals of sexuality in old people.

What is happening now is that people are going to live in
sheltered accommodation and, if sex rears its ugly head, the
social workers can be horrified and appalled and can even use
unpleasant epithets about it. But they could begin to think that it
is rather nice that loving goes on into old age, and the point
about it is that everybody going to live in sheltered accommodation is still a sexual person. Provision must be made for
them. They must have privacy and the right to a private life. And
if they happen to see somebody they like in the same
accommodation they must have room made available to them to
be together, to be private.

She began to get involved in community issues during the Second
World War. Her daughter having been evacuated at the beginning of
the war, she went out and joined the Women's Voluntary Service and
worked in a variety of jobs, first in canteens and then as an assistant to
a matron in a hospital where old people were evacuated. 'In those
days it was really a form of social work', she says.

Jane's health broke down during the war, and so she was excused
war work and went back to her home. But, by the end of the war, her
health had improved and she decided that she did not want to stay at
home any longer. She became involved in a campaign to retain the
nurseries which had opened during the war to allow women to
become involved in factory work.

They were open from eight in the morning to six in the evening.
In Liverpool we had many one-parent families and because it
was a big seaport we had a lot of deserted wives, so we had a lot
of women needing nursery accommodation. After the war, the
general idea was to close them all. All the big cities mounted
campaigns to keep them open. I was friendly with one or two
Labour councillors who formed a committee to keep them open.
They invited me to be secretary and we had a six-month
campaign and we kept them as a result of it. I visited every day
nursery and organised public meetings, and we had the matrons
and the mums with the kids on the platforms. Not only did we
keep them, but we managed to keep the cost down as well.

Jane says she began to get involved in politics at around this time,
mainly as a result of listening to her daughter, then 15 years old, and
her friends talking about the causes of war: 'I used to listen to the kids
sitting around on the floor wondering what the devil I could give

them to eat in the evenings. And I realised that what they were talking about ought to be my business – the causes of war and poverty.'

In fact, in 1944 she joined the Communist Party and quickly became an activist. In the early 1950s, much of her time was spent in the fledgling peace movement, protesting at the threat of German rearmament: 'I took a leading part as a member of the peace council and I used to go around to co-operative guilds and women's organisations talking about the peace movement and on all the demonstrations. We'd take busloads of mothers down to London to protest at rearmament.'

Jane joined a community association in Penny Lane, near her home, and for several years this became the focus of her life.

In this I found the body I liked. There were men and women of all ages. We had all kinds of interesting diversions – dancing and cards, and so on. We had classes as well and a discussion group which was the largest group in the centre. The centre itself was an old building left empty after the war. The council for social services had money left by the Americans for community work, and the education committee thought it would be a good idea to open an experimental community centre.

Hundreds of people regularly attended the activities of the centre, the most popular event being the discussion group. The council for social services was very proud of the association and any dignitaries visiting Liverpool would be brought round to see it in action. Ultimately, Jane became chairwoman of the discussion group and 50 or 60 people would attend most weeks, with more than 100 on special occasions. 'We used to have mock parliaments and things like that', says Jane.

But, by the early 1950s, the mood in the country had begun to change. Fewer people came to the association's meetings and it began to stagnate. Then the building was found to be unsafe and much to Jane's regret, the association had to close down. But she was undismayed and decided to continue the same kind of work by becoming a member of another association in West Derby. She was co-opted on to the executive and from there on to the national executive of the National Federation of Community Organisations (NFCO) in 1959, 'partly because I was a woman and, although most of the work in the associations was being done by women, there were hardly any on the national executive'.

This was the start of a hectic period in Jane's life, attending regular monthly meetings at the Bedford Square offices in London of the old National Council for Social Services (forerunner of the National Council for Voluntary Organisations – NVCO) where the NFCO was based at that time. She travelled extensively round the country attending conferences and meetings throughout the late 1950s and early 1960s.

But, once again, changes in community work and public attitudes had their effect.

Very strangely, community work began to fall away in Liverpool. It was mainly due to a change in local government, I think. We had had a Conservative council and they supported community work. They gave grants to community associations and we had peripatetic community wardens. But when the Liberals came in they didn't support us. They wanted community work, but linked to their party. The result was that people drifted away.

Jane kept up her interests in her local community, but the national aspect of her work fell away. Little changed for several years until 1974 when she and her family were hit by a terrible tragedy. Her daughter was killed in a hit-and-run accident, shortly after leaving the house.

It was a dreadful loss. She left two children and we were an absolutely decimated family. She was a much-loved social worker and ahead of her time. Her memory is now honoured in Liverpool. There is a Sheila Kay Day Centre, and there is a fund her friends subscribed to and John Moores Jnr [the pools millionaire] subscribed a large sum of money. It is an educational fund, originally to provide money to girls who had left school without passing an exam and then, later on in life, wanted to take on some form of education – a second chance to learn.

The fund pays for such items as childminding costs and fees for conferences, and is now also open to young men.

For a while, Jane was in 'a bit of a wilderness'. Life was very difficult and she was very unhappy but, after about a year, she began to bounce back. Her husband retired (she herself was 71 by this time) and had become depressed, as he was suffering from eye problems and was convinced that he was going to go blind. Life became difficult at home: 'We began to argue and bicker about detail.'

Then one day in 1979 she had a telephone call from a lecturer at Liverpool University.

She said the students had been to see people living in sheltered accommodation and they had realised there was no provision for privacy and wanted to know why. No one appeared to have asked before. There was nothing in the literature about it. They asked her if elderly people had a need for sexual relations and she had to say she did not know. Alex Comfort had not written his book about the joy of sex at that time. The students asked for an old person who might talk, you see, and that's why they approached me. I've been doing it for 10 years now and it has led to other things.

Three years ago, the Institute of Human Ageing at the University of Liverpool asked Jane to speak at their annual general meeting as the final speaker on the subject of celebrating age. She was given a standing ovation after her speech, and it was printed by the Institute: 'In fact, I'm still doing that talk – I did it this morning.'

She also now gives a talk on how to stretch an old-age pension: 'I've become a bit of an authority on that and I seem to get lots of requests. I'm going to Gloucester next Tuesday to speak to an Age Concern gathering and next Friday I'm going to Barrow to speak there.'

Life has never been busier for Jane. Her only worry now is that other old people need to be persuaded to do what she does.

I'm constantly saying to the Institute and other people, 'Why don't you try and turn some other older people into speakers?' because, if I turn my toes up tomorrow, it's going to leave a gap, I know. It's just purely fortuitous that someone asked me to speak and I got up and found that I could do it. I think women make good communicators. They talk ordinary language. I think what I'm doing is active citizenship because I talk about reality and I do bring in a bit of politics. I say we are 10 million and that we could make our opinion known at the ballot box. I tell them that they have a responsibility and that there is such a thing as grey power.

Jane is unlikely to slow down as long as her health remains good. She lost her husband in May 1989 and, although that has affected her, she has kept up her appointments.

I've got enough engagements to see me through to next March. I quite expect the time will come when I will have to say 'no', but it's not yet. Because I get a lot out of doing it – enormous satisfaction and self-esteem. And I'm persuaded it is very necessary. But I do keep saying that you should encourage other women as well.

CHAPTER 3

LALITA AHMED

*I had the opportunity because people came and asked me . . . Also
I had time . . . and I did not have to count the pennies. Also I had
an inborn desire to help.*

Lalita Ahmed arrived in Britain to live 29 years ago. Having left
university in India with a science degree, she was recruited to become
the first television presenter on Indian television. A scholarship to
study production techniques in the United States followed and, as a
result of that, she came to England and shortly after decided to settle
down.

Almost from the time she arrived in Britain, she has been active in a
wide variety of voluntary organisations, mostly, but not exclusively,
connected to the Asian community in Britain. 'I've never counted,
but there must be about 200 organisations that I have been connected
with over the years,' she says.

Lalita comes from a Brahmin family and so is a Hindu, but she
married a Moslem. She says she and her husband would have found it
difficult to stay in either Pakistan or India and, in some ways, she
says, 'it was like marrying a German during the Second World War'.
Both countries had been at war with each other.

However, her family did not object to the marriage, although she
was given a serious talking-to by her parents: 'I was told the pros and
cons. It was very unusual at that time, particularly because of the
politics. In some ways we were very glad to be in England where we
could settle down and work at our marriage.'

To further complicate the picture, Lalita was educated at a
Catholic convent in India: 'My mother thought it gave a better
religious background than the Protestant or Anglican schools did.
She wanted religion to be in our life.' In fact, four generations of
Lalita's family have been educated at Christian schools in India,
starting with her grandfather.

My father was an accountant with the railways. He always insisted on a first class education, because we come from a very poor family and my father wanted us to do well. There is a saying in India that you can take wealth away, but you can never take an education that is in your stomach. Nobody can steal that.

She has, in part, continued that tradition, sending her son for part of his education to a Catholic school, despite the fact that all three children have been brought up as Moslems. 'We thought that our children would have a very great understanding of Christianity and that they could balance between these three great religions. We all believe in one God and it doesn't matter how you worship as long as you believe. The teachings are all similar.'

Not long after arriving in Britain, Lalita began working for the BBC for *Gharbar*, the first programme on British TV for Asians. That was in 1967 when an influx of Asian refugees from East Africa had begun to arrive.

It was very basic at that time. We used to do little items about how people could use the gas and electricity, hot-water geysers, and so on. How to dress, go to the doctor's, what benefits people could claim. It gradually evolved into looking at the problems of Asian women, how they should bring up children, how to run a creche, or get involved in adult education. Another issue which I began to raise at that time, but which was very much out of favour, was the idea of mother-tongue lessons for children. The government was opposed, but how can a mother have a proper relationship with her own children unless she can address them in her own language?

Lalita always worked on a part-time or freelance basis and soon found that there were many issues in which she could become involved. 'When you come from a poor country you want to help. So I got myself involved with the early immigrants who were coming from East Africa. There were lots of organisations at that time which would crop up and maybe only last for a year or so.'

She was involved in helping to set up and run the Southall Women's Association and the Southall Asian Youth Movement. Lalita also served as chairwoman for two terms of the UK Asian Women's Conference, having run the branch in New Malden, where she now lives.

We first fought against the immigration laws. Every year there was a new law or amendment to stop Asians coming to this country. We fought very vigorously with the government. We were given a grant from the Equal Opportunities Commission to help set up an office and my husband gave us free accommodation and running expenses to meet the costs. Through that we became members of the Swann Committee, police advisory bodies, the Prisoners' Wives Association and we were able to set up two Asian women's centres – one in Brixton and another in Coventry.

Another organisation set up around the same time was Sangam, in which Lalita was very active. Sangam means the meeting point of two rivers or, more colloquially, getting together. She helped set up a legal department which, for the first time, was able to give legal advice to women who had become divorced, separated, or widowed. Sangam also runs English classes and provides lecturers on all aspects of social life.

Lalita, as befits someone with her own heterodox background, has also given help to members of other Asian communities, such as the Jain Youth Movement, Millan (a Sindhi community organisation), and for Bengalis in Newham. She was even made an honorary member of an Islamic women's organisation in Northampton. 'Because I am not 100 per cent sure of my understanding of Islam I thought I might offend them, so it never went much further than that,' she says.

Besides her work for social organisations, Lalita is also very involved with Asian arts organisations. She was a chairwoman of the Asian Music Academy in Clapham and is still a trustee. She is also a trustee of the Academy of Indian Music and Dance at The Place in London.

Her background in TV and radio has also caused her to be much in demand from a wide range of charities and voluntary organisations who have used her journalistic skills in a number of programmes: in particular, for the Asian Mother and Baby Campaign, for whom she helped to make a number of documentaries.

She also served on the committee of the Think British Campaign which started in 1980.

I worked for about three years with them. It started with British companies, but they were very keen to get to the immigrant communities. Most companies were not serving the immigrant communities at all. The foods were not there, nor the clothes. All of it was being imported. Even butter to make ghee was being imported, as was flour. I told them they must not neglect the Asian community because we are basically traders. It was very important that Asians should think of themselves as being citizens of this country and not forever immigrants who have come from abroad and they are only here to make money and go back.

The campaign aimed to encourage Asians to use English fruit and vegetables and showed them how to make ghee with English butter. 'Eat English and make this country prosperous, was the message', she says.

The list of Lalita's activities is enormous. She also helps to fund an orphanage in Calcutta at Khela Ghar, which was set up after the war between Pakistan and Bangladesh. Each year she tries to reach her target by raising money from Asian businessmen in Britain. And, locally, she is closely involved with an old people's home in New Malden, taking the residents out shopping three times a week.

I had always lived in an extended family close to my mother, mother-in-law and maternal grandmother. I saw what a wonderful role they contribute, whereas here they are all discarded like old shoes. I don't agree with that. They should not be hidden away in old people's homes. All their lives they contribute to the betterment of the nation and the welfare of their children and just at the time when they are most vulnerable and weak and need love, nobody gives it to them. I would very much like the Indian system brought into this country. The children are forced by law to look after them. They should be. Their needs are very few, but they are starved of affection.

Lalita's particular interest in women's issues stems from her perception of the way in which women are particularly affected by their social isolation and customs.

I have always been particularly involved in Asian women's problems, because I really saw them suffer. They had no platform whereby they could speak for themselves. First, there was the language problem. Second, there were very few women who had the advantage I had, who had the support of a husband to go out and speak. I also had the opportunity because people came and asked me. Because there are many talented women here, but people do not know them. Also I had time, I could drive a car and I did not have to count the pennies too closely. Also I had an inborn desire to help.

She was also briefly associated with the Bengali International Women's Association, an organisation which points to the remarkable changes that have come about amongst Bengali women in Britain. 'There are some magnificent women doing a tremendous amount of work,' she says.

The other issues connected to Asian women are the dowry system – 'trading women for material gain' as she puts it – and arranged marriages. Lalita was involved in this latter issue, although she emphasises that the good aspect of the system is seldom highlighted, namely the high success rate. 'But it is the 25 per cent of such marriages that don't work that are really upsetting', she says. 'Briefly I was involved in it, but I 'had to come out. It broke my heart. I became so depressed and I am not that strong, so I had to leave it.'

Lalita feels that her desire to help stems from her education in India.

I never felt I was in a foreign country when I came here, because I knew so much English history through my education. My whole family knows English history inside out. The thing that surprised me was that the idea of English people I had brought with me from India was so great, I was totally disillusioned when I came here. There were no manners here, I didn't like the way people lived, the way they only thought of themselves. It took me a number of years to really understand the way English people were.

This was partly because in India she had been exposed to a different (some might say one-sided) view of English culture. But the fact that Lalita did not feel overawed by English culture – and, indeed, felt considerable pride in her own Indian-ness – gave her a lot of confidence.

I wasn't afraid if an English lady turned around and said 'Paki go home', because I could tell her a few things myself. Maybe that confidence also contributed to my motivation in that I could tell the Asian community, 'If you contribute fully to the welfare of this country and make it your country, then you don't

always have to be under pressure and subservient to the local
people.'

But Lalita makes one important proviso – that immigrants in general
should accept that they are here to stay.

This is my first condition. If you feel for this place as your home
the way I feel – I mean, I am prepared to fight anybody. I would
fight for this country if it came to that. It doesn't come easily to
say that at every step of the way you are made to feel an
immigrant, a sponger, and that is a very hard feeling to shake.

Citizenship for most immigrants is usually understood in the
context of legal rights of abode and entry. The question of civic rights
is much more confused. Many feel that they are outside civic society,
even if they are legally full citizens. That is why Lalita stresses the
importance of taking a decision to stay in Britain for good.

If their loyalty is divided, then they are only here to take
advantage of the good things this country has to offer. I am sure
there is quite a large number of people who feel that one day they
will go back and that is what stops them from participating in a
substantial way.

She points out that for the second and third generations this issue will
be easier.

The second generation is here to stay and many of the first
generation are going to die in this country with the dream in their
heart that one day they will go back. I don't see any sign that they
will. The third generation will have the most difficult task. You
see, we came with many dreams and mostly fulfilled them. The
second generation was made to live our dreams and we didn't
allow them to become 100 per cent British. We held on to them.
But they are only able to pass on to their children an *idea* of India
or Pakistan, because they have never experienced it. They have
had a mixed culture . . . But when they have children they will
have very little of that Indian-ness to pass on.

Lalita's own family illustrates the point. Her children, born and
educated in Britain and with an outlook that is almost entirely
British, felt out of place when in India. The issues which concern them

are not so much the ones which directly affect their community, but the wider, global issues such as pollution, famine and the environment.

For Lalita, citizenship in the civic sense of the word has meant playing a full part in the welfare of her community and taking an active interest in British social issues. 'Apart from whatever was necessary to give to my family, I have contributed every remaining minute for the betterment of my community.' Looking at the list of causes she has been associated with, no one could doubt it for a moment.

CHAPTER 4

DAVID BRYAN

I think it is still possible to encourage people to be active. The process is by having groups like ourselves able to be the mechanism by which people can actually find a point of entry.

South London's largest and most exciting black arts and cultural centre is to be found in the heart of Brixton in Lambeth's Peace Gardens. The former St Matthew's Church, built with classical portico in 1824 as one of the four Waterloo churches, and fallen into disrepair by the mid-1900s, was renovated under the government urban aid programme to the tune of £2.5 million, to provide a six-storey, multi-purpose complex for the local community.

'Brixton Village' was launched in January 1986 under the stimulus of David Bryan, a charismatic young black activist from Brixton.

I see myself as an agent of change, someone who actually takes on the responsibility to make something happen, and with this project over the last five years it's been about changing people's ideas about community involvement in a community development context, showing that we can participate in a positive way and that riots are not necessarily a component of change – although they have their influence – and, at the same time, influencing young people to have more confidence in themselves so that they, too, can achieve more in life.

David's idea was to develop an innovative programme which would reflect the cultural diversity of the community and provide a focus for the large Afro-Caribbean population. When the project started, 15 years earlier, the aim was to have a multi-purpose community centre. But it took 13 years to convert the building, and during that time the social milieu changed:

We moved from being a responsive church hall type setting where groups came to us. During the giddy days of the seventies when groups were in abundance and money was also flourishing that was fine, because groups could pay a nominal sum, and we could act as administrators and caretakers. But, as the groups vanished, we had to rethink our role, and I came in at that juncture and said, 'Look, we have to take a proactive stance because to sit back and wait for things to change externally is not going to be to our benefit.'

The result was that the emphasis was put on community development, through the arts and cultural expression. This is not surprising given that the Village boasts a magnificent 250-seat theatre and dressing rooms, professional rehearsal space, conference and exhibition rooms and its own private chapel.

David views this transformation as a contribution to community regeneration. It was partly about 'trying to establish a presence so that the nation could know that Brixton Village existed and provides a range of cultural expressions for everyone'. As the Village handout explains,

Brixton Village would cater from the cradle to the grave. One could be christened, attend the Playgroup, be baptised, attend a children's festival, undertake supplementary education through the Saturday school, go to the disco, attend a range of plays reflecting cultures of the world, aspire to be a stage producer or centre director.

Brixton Village was seen as a natural progression from a voluntary community project to a cultural centre, born out of the need to reflect, express and record the Caribbean cultural experience in Britain.

What we have said is that we will try to respond directly to the community and, by the community's turn-out to events, clearly we have struck a chord ... We have proven as a new theatre, in a new arena, that black people actually want to go out and see theatre, when many people thought before that we didn't. ... So we have educated a whole sector of the arts facility now that the market is bigger than they had previously anticipated and understood.

But he is concerned that they should not be ghettoised, and seen as only for the black community, and that they should represent a fairly wide range of arts that the community otherwise would not get access to. For this reason, they hope to key into international theatre and film festivals. But primarily,

> We came in with a concern for promoting the black community in Brixton, because everybody sees Brixton as being a black community, and the mythology is difficult to alter. We were trying to create a positive image of the black community within that community. To do this we wanted to give them something which said 'look, we are proud of what we are, what we contribute to the general life of this country' and, at the same time, offer an example to other boroughs, other places.

He believes that they have succeeded in this, for they are viewed with pride and praised by the community for the work they have done, their events are well supported and their facilities are well used. In 1988 they hosted their first and highly successful Caribbean theatre season, and hope in the future to break into film and video production and even make a joint bid for their own community radio station.

David's starting point in community development came early. Born of Jamaican parents, he attended a comprehensive school in Tulse Hill at a time when the black community was beginning to assert itself and black power was becoming a strong force and presence.

> I was in my teens in 1968 at the peak point of black power in America, and that was an international phenomenon, and therefore we were watching the runners at the Olympics with their clenched fists and there was a phenomenal feeling of pride, of assertion. We were reading books by Martin Luther King, Malcolm X and others, even the Panthers.

What came out of that was not so much a 'hard-nosed radicalism, anti-white stance', although there was a tinge of that, but rather the discovery that they had a history. 'It is hard to imagine now, because everybody claims to be enlightened about the need for such things. But if you cast your mind back to the sixties, people were still being lynched in the States quite openly.' At an English school the pupils never heard about the Caribbean or Africa; it was not considered relevant. They learnt English and European history, the Reformation and the Second World War. He knows it inside out. He had to teach himself Caribbean history, Asian history, and he and his fellow black pupils became active in pursuing their own history in school after hours. They involved other local schools in coming to Tulse Hill sixth form and debating the facts which they were discovering.

> We were all sitting there with textbooks, pupils doing it, no teachers in sight, hundreds of us at times because we all came in. We brought in outside speakers to help us elaborate on concepts, and that is how we began to teach ourselves. So from there I saw the need for self-learning, self-development, because clearly agencies were not doing so and not from an informed world-view perspective.

There was resistance to this 'for very dubious reasons'. And now, as people are beginning to talk about 1992, he feels 'we should really be thinking about what we are teaching our kids in terms of their world opportunities'. To do this 'it is best that they have respect for and understand other cultures and histories and therefore can engage them with meaning'.

After he left school, David tried to create institutions that could help fight racism and perpetuate such an awareness, and so became involved in community publishing, bookshops and arts, as in his present job. It was all an endeavour to say to his community, 'don't be despondent, don't diminish your opportunities or your abilities by lack of confidence'.

Up until the mid-1970s some of his fellow pupils stuck with the issue as he did, then found that they could not earn a living in that environment.

> Doors were still closed in our faces, our experiences were still said to be not relevant enough to other agencies in the mainstream. So many of them went off into teaching, into becoming lawyers, into various other professions, and became absorbed in them.

He thinks that they still continue to be active for their communities in small ways and knows, if he calls on them from time to time, that they are more than willing to help out. And he believes that, in their particular areas of work, they are still trying to pursue the awareness of the importance of black culture as much as the boundaries of their work will allow. But the voluntary sector is too fragile and too precarious for most people.

The main problem, of course, is funding. The board outside 'Brixton Village' states: 'Another Lambeth Community Project. Helped by money from the Government's Urban Programme.' When David arrived in 1984 the project was 95 per cent dependent on Lambeth Council for funds. That annual grant of £75,000 was axed in July 1988 and, after that, the staff had to raise their own salaries. They now generate close to 70 per cent of their income, and other funding agencies make up the difference.

The income is raised by hiring out space for theatre rehearsals, committees, conferences, weddings, annual general meetings, weekend discos and local community groups. But this means that they are restricted to local organisations that can afford to pay, and are not available to small new groups without funds.

David's experience with Lambeth Council has not been a happy one.

> I have seen five leaders of the local Labour Party and, when you have that kind of fluctuation, it's difficult as a community voluntary project to know what support you can glean from the local authority, because you are not sure what its strategy is, if it has one.

He says that he has been regarded as too forthright and critical, and his entrepreneurial schemes have been dismissed by the council as 'yuppy'. Some of the plays he has put on have upset various groups, including feminists. The council have objected to the price of his theatre tickets being too high. They have closed a black community nursery that David was an adviser to for what, he feels, were political reasons and also because they said the weekly rates of £25 were too much. He says that he will not subscribe to the notion that black equals poor, or that 'we just suffer the disadvantage caused by racism'.

Because he realised that no more funding would be forthcoming from the council while he was director, David decided to leave Brixton Village at the end of September 1989. But he wanted to stick with the issue of black culture

> because I think that my generation who were influenced by the sixties – who were able to look at political issues before political debates outside party politics were thought to be variant and

extreme – have got a sense of history and community which isn't easily acquired now . . . As much as schools talk about multi-culturalism and therefore have a degree of input into our history, and as much as it is now easier to buy books by black writers and everybody is reading them, it is important to remember the time when those things were not allowed at all, when Lenny Henry could never have got on TV and had his own show and be thought to be a universal image. There's still more to be achieved and we can't become complacent.

He does not believe that the context in which the black community is trying to make its impact is only one of isolation and separatism. But he feels that black people came willingly to this country to integrate into the economic fabric of society and were rejected. They came to integrate and share their culture and it was marginalised. He believes that current successes can easily evaporate tomorrow. What has happened to the issue of racism is a good example of this.

It has diminished out of the mainstream agenda. In some ways that's good because it means one doesn't have to get anxious that, at every party political campaign or conference, they are going to make Nationality Acts an issue . . . but it assumes that racism doesn't exist any longer, and that is far from the case . . . I think we need somehow to identify that there are serious issues – of women, of race, of age, of care for children – that don't need to be today's spectacular issues but must be continuous ones, because resources go towards the things that are not suffering from media fatigue today.

So what has he achieved at Brixton Village? He feels they have established their own black community 'that proves that the local people can create, and are creating, a contribution for all against the indifference of local authorities and many others who allow doubt to cloud their judgement'. The local people have made it clear that this is the place which they want to have, to own it themselves, 'and to say we have made something happen and made it work, even though the odds have been quite considerable'.

It used to be community development I was most involved in – nurturing local groups, aiding development, aiding discussions with a variety of agencies about given issues, be it educational, be it the elderly, or just general community work. But over the

last couple of years, I have moved more and more into the area
of the arts and cultural expression.

The Village has recently started a membership scheme and is trying
to work out other ideas to allow the public to participate in the centre
and its direction in a positive way.

I think it is still possible to encourage people to be active. The
process is by having groups like ourselves able to be the
mechanism by which people can actually find a point of entry
and something they can learn through. It's about having the
space and the resources and having faith. It's a kind of group
work, it's counselling, it's being there when it matters, it's
phoning up and saying, 'how has the exam gone?' It's not
presuming that everyone that's black is involved in drugs. It's
setting a very positive, optimistic view and pushing an individual
gently, but steadily.

He knows that he is in largely uncharted territory:

There hasn't been an organisation in England (unlike America)
to debate the issue of creating black institutions and the role they
can play without seeing them as being antagonistic, confronta-
tional and separatist. There hasn't been a proper debate about
what is black culture, and how that can be nurtured.

When he joined the project at the age of 26, there was no one else of
his age working in the field, and he has had to learn as he went along.
But if no one had given him the opportunity, he would not have
learnt. David Bryan is continuing his commitment to black
community development and the arts in his present role as an
independent management consultant advising small organisations,
as well as regional organisations with funding responsibilities. He
feels that 'Our abilities to lead and influence our own destiny and that
of society for the benefit of all must be asserted, otherwise we will
always be seen and treated as less than equal.'

CHAPTER 5

FEMI OTITOJU

Perhaps the most important thing . . . is questioning what happens
to us, the effect that central government, local government and
other community organisations have on us, and how we feel about
that.

Femi Otitoju's house in Muswell Hill, with its black and yellow
furnishings, abundant plants and poster of Grace Jones, reflects her
temperament – confident, assertive and joyous. Femi is one of 120
volunteers who work on the London Lesbian and Gay Switchboard.
What is unusual is that not only is she the only black lesbian there, but
that in August 1989 she was elected as their chair.

Femi does not necessarily think of herself as an active citizen, she
just sees herself as someone who does not sit down and let things
happen to her. She thinks that it means taking charge of your own
life, and ideally helping other people to take charge of their lives as
well: 'Perhaps the most important thing in all of that is questioning
what happens to us, the effect that central government, local
government and other community organisations have on us, and how
we feel about that.'

The activities which she is involved in are mainly the issues that
affect her personally – lesbian and gay rights, black issues right across
the board (working mainly with other black women), and the
women's movement.

The spur to getting involved was being brought up alone by her
mother, and not understanding why she would get so cross about not
being able to buy a washing machine on the 'never never' like
everybody else could. 'It was realising it was because in those days she
didn't have a man and I didn't have a daddy.' During the school term,
she was brought up in Worthing by white English foster parents and
in the holidays by her mother, a Nigerian woman with a strong
identity with her cultural roots who had left her husband in Nigeria to

return to the UK to finish studying law. From then on, Femi felt that life ought to be easier for women and that they should not be penalised for living alone, as her mother was.

Late in her school career, she had a very dynamic headmistress who had never married and was very powerful and enigmatic. Femi decided that she would be like her. Even then, she did not know what avenue she would take. Then, as she was about to go to university, she picked up a copy of *Spare Rib* and thought 'Goodness, this is it, here we have everything I've been thinking.' She decided not to go to university 'because I'd discovered all these incredible women who were doing amazing things'. They talked a lot about the situation of women, and agreed that they did not just have to grin and bear it.

At this time, she was interested in developing her feminist and political views. Her sexuality had never been a problem. She had been to bed with her girlfriend at an early age and she thought that, if she waited, other girls would start talking about what they did with their girlfriends. They didn't. But, as her sexuality had never been squashed, it did not seem something she needed to fight about: 'Whereas being a woman, being allowed to do three A-level sciences, was something I had to fight for.'

Femi 'chugged along being part of the women's movement' (and to an extent of the lesbian movement), adding the seventh demand – a woman's right to define her own sexuality – to the six demands of the women's liberation movement. She had happily settled down with a woman and was working from 9 to 5 to get money. Then she met a gay man who spent a year trying to persuade her to get involved in Gay Switchboard. Finally, she decided to join what she then felt was an extremely male-dominated organisation.

So she became one of four women alongside 80 men, and the only black woman on the Switchboard. She found it very exhilarating. 'I was in the organisation for two years before anyone even asked me to make them a cup of tea. They wouldn't dare. And that was great.' It was then that she first began to become a public figure in the lesbian and gay movement – now she is 'quite high profile'.

In 1989, she went to the second ever black lesbian conference – there were about 500 women there – and was very struck by the high percentage of women who were of Nigerian descent rather than Afro-Caribbean. She wonders whether this is related to the fact that the first black lesbian who had a high profile in the black community was a Nigerian. It made her feel that everyone has a real responsibility 'because you can just make things so much easier for others if they have someone they can identify with'. One 80-year-old woman at the conference, whose husband had died, described how she had discovered her sexuality two years before when she read a magazine called *Square Peg* in the doctor's surgery and followed up the phone numbers.

Femi says that she now gives Switchboard the equivalent of a working week a month. She has also been involved in the Stonewall Housing Association (a lesbian and gay housing association), training for the Black Lesbian and Gay Phoneline, helping to organise the black lesbian and gay international conference and leafletting for the local Labour Party.

Femi has been fortunate to find ways of earning a living which have allowed her to express her beliefs. She worked 'very successfully' for two years for the Greater London Council, empowering and resourcing various women's organisations. Then she joined Haringey Council as one of the first workers in the lesbian and gay unit. It was the first such unit in the country, and she eventually spent two years training people around the issue of heterosexism.

Now she works as a freelance trainer and consultant on equal opportunities: 'It feels like a continuation of all the work that I do in the voluntary sector because I don't change my manner, I don't change my style, and I certainly don't change what I'm aiming to achieve.' She works for local authorities, voluntary sector organisations, and a little bit for the private sector.

What has enabled Femi to 'come out', get involved and make her sexuality an integral part of her life?

It's partly about being displaced, about being different, and not having any choice about that, and so not being afraid to continue to be different. I don't have an option to blend in. You can't blend in when you're six foot tall, and black, with a very very very English accent. I certainly couldn't blend in in Worthing. I couldn't blend in as the only black kid in the grammar school I was at. And I've always felt different. I've always been a lesbian. So I have no fear of being different.

There's a certain social mobility, too. My mother considers herself very upper class. My foster parents were British working class, 10p in the gas meter and no money on Thursdays before pay day. And I spent my years going between the two. So there was nowhere I don't belong. I think that's about circumstance and environment, and obviously some of it has to be about character, and general make-up – who I am and what I am.

She says that Yoruba women have a reputation for being really stroppy women: 'In fact, we mooted maybe that's why there are so many Yoruba lesbians about – because we tend not to put up with the rubbish.' She thinks that her vibrancy comes from being a Nigerian woman, and that the tenacity is her own. She is not easily squashed, and has 'terrible habits, which get me into all kinds of trouble, but in terms of moving forward with my community they are wonderful'. They mainly concern never being frightened to ask for what she wants, and never taking 'no' for an answer.

Her mother is also tenacious and Femi believes that she takes after her in the way she operates. There is one example of this from her childhood that remains very vivid in her memory and she often uses it in her training.

> I remember being taken to a shoeshop because the heel had fallen off my shoe while I was walking along and my mother saying, 'We want another pair of shoes.' And they didn't have a suitable pair in stock and they said 'You'll have to find something, won't you, because she hasn't got any shoes to wear', and my mother said, 'Oh will we?' and I remember, as a child, being made to wear two plastic carrier bags on my legs with elastic bands round my ankles walking out of the shop because she wasn't going to be bulldozed by this shopkeeper.

She cannot see any problem in encouraging others to become more active and get involved in things, because she believes that bringing about the process of change is addictive.

> Once you realise that something's happened because you wanted it, it was your idea, and that you brought it through ... or that it brings good to other people – sometimes the buzz isn't about glory glory, it's about 'that is so fab, that I've done for somebody else'. So I think it is possible to encourage other people, and that has to be about having recognisable and achievable goals, and getting people's involvement on the edges of things, so there are little things they feel they can cope with.

She remembers some of the Section 28 rallies (against a proposed law to ban the 'promotion' of homosexuality by local authorities):

> We all got on a train and we drank this pink fizz which gave us a hangover by 11 o'clock, and got off the train and walked for

miles, and got back on the train and came back to London and that was supposed to be a success. But I didn't feel that I'd achieved, and I'm sure lots of other people didn't feel they'd achieved, and I'm sure next time they'll remember the hangover and the drudge, as there was no buzz to remember.

Whereas one of the most effective ways of dealing with Section 28 was to tackle individuals or groups of people in your own community, as they did in Haringey. Just four of them actually stopped a particular councillor coming into a meeting on the issue, and that *was* an achievement. It was also better in terms of encouraging people and keeping them.

She applied the same kind of methods to Gay Switchboard which was in the process of buying a new building at the time of her interview. Not all 120 volunteers needed to be involved in the purchase, but all needed to feel that there was at least one aspect that they were going to be a part of.

So everyone is divided up into sub-groups, and we're going to be looking at the decor, and we're going to be looking at the layout, and we're going to be looking at the uses different rooms will be put to, so everyone at the end can feel, 'I did that, that was my contribution'.

After 15 years of existence, London Lesbian and Gay Switchboard now runs up to 5 lines for 24 hours a day. Femi's aim when she is on the line is to get callers to feel good about the possibility that they might be gay, to let them know what their next step might be and, ideally, to leave them with some kind of continuing involvement within the lesbian and gay community.

So the structure of the call might be somebody saying they think they might be gay, working out how they feel about being gay, trying to allay any fears that they express and countering the rubbish they will have heard elsewhere. And then to work out what level of support they've got or what possible levels of support there are, because sometimes people don't recognise them. 'I tell my sister about absolutely everything.' 'Well, why don't you try telling her this?' It may not have occurred to them. And then to look at ways they could connect with their local lesbian and gay community, depending on their own lifestyle and geographical location.

Femi thinks that she would always have been a lesbian, but she would not necessarily have lived as a lesbian if different things had happened to her – for example, if her mother had not had the experience she did:

It's perfectly possible I would be married with two kids and having affairs with women down the road, but desperately quiet and not a lesbian in the way I mean by it. So I'm a lesbian because there was room for me and because I was lucky. I was lucky to find the women's movement at the stage in my life when I did . . . It's a driving force, my sexuality, as basic as hunger. It was there before I even knew what it was.

As far as the women's movement is concerned she says:

Well, it's resting, isn't it? My emphasis at the moment is about coalition-building, about looking at the links between oppressed groups, and the things we have in common – and that's partly because I belong to so many of the oppressed groups that it's in my interest to have all these organisations working together! One of the emphases that I put forward in my work is about links around disability, community and black communities, and so on. I think that is really where the new force in the women's movement is going to come from.

I think it's a mistake on the part of some feminists to say that it is the other equality issues that are diluting the women's movement. The reality is that the women's movement has neglected those issues really quite abysmally, and that is one of the reasons why women are now going more for autonomy. It used to be enough to be part of the women's movement, but when that movement is ablist [that is, discriminates against women with disabilities], and is racist, you do draw away to a subsection, and I think we need to recognise that if we don't build bridges, these sections will go off all over the place. But the women's movement isn't over at all.

I'm surprised, really, that we didn't riot around Section 28. I actually would have taken to the streets. I think we are getting angrier, but we're not angry enough yet.

CHAPTER 6

CHRISTINE CARDWELL

*If you choose to take control of your life . . . you can grow,
and one of the very rewarding things about working in Women's
Aid . . . is that some women . . . do go through that process.*

The south side of the city of Glasgow has changed beyond all
recognition in the past 10 years. There is a splendid new mosque just
south of the Clyde. Most of the Gorbals has been pulled down. Now,
high-rise blocks tower over waste land, but it is only recently that the
planners have realised that these are just as much prisons as the
delapidated buildings which they were intended to replace.

Other mainly low-rise estates have sprung up, some, such as
Castlemill, on a gigantic scale. In this, once the biggest estate in
Europe, 60,000 people inhabit an area virtually deprived of shops and
amenities – a situation made worse by chronic unemployment among
its inhabitants. In such conditions, it is often the women who bear the
major burden.

Christine Cardwell lives a stone's throw from Castlemill with
Donald and their two sons aged 20 and 12. 'Communities such as
Castlemill are crippled', she says, 'but materially, not in the human
spirit.'

Her concern about women's rights issues has led her to get involved
in the women's self-defence network and, for the past two years, to be
a paid, part-time training and development worker in Hamilton
Women's Aid. This offers refuge, if possible, and safe houses to
abused women and their children, plus information and advice on
legal rights. They also respond to local demand by doing other
outreach work such as giving talks and skills training.

There are 37 women's aid groups in Scotland, including Shetland,
and Christine insists that is nowhere near enough. They are funded in
different ways. Hamilton is funded 75 per cent by Urban Aid, 12 per
cent by the regional authority, and 12½ per cent by the district

council. Funding is very shaky for some groups and they have to try and get money from wherever they can – even more so in the last couple of years due to government cuts. The lack of importance given to voluntary groups, particularly those working with women and children, has affected the whole climate in which such work is undertaken.

Her involvement in women's self-defence is a voluntary contribution which she does mainly through the Workers' Educational Association. She says that there is an enormous demand for self-defence skills in the West of Scotland from women of all ages, able and disabled, which it is impossible to meet. So they are constantly struggling to develop materials, develop support groups and offer classes or courses for women. But it is not always successful – and very slow.

> It's a very particular form of self-defence where the physical aspect is no more important than the discussion and the awareness raising. All the materials and the resources we use come from a feminist reference whereby it's very clear that we're unhappy at needing self-defence, and the responsibility for any type of violence lies with the men that perpetrate it. It includes assertiveness work and some very basic physical techniques. But I think the real strengths of the work are breaking isolation, helping women to talk in a safe atmosphere, and sometimes disclose abuse that they have never had the chance to speak about.

Once they've been through this course, the women may go on to do a range of things such as keep fit, or lobbying local councillors for street lighting. Self-defence for women got off the ground in Glasgow in 1983 when a woman came from Aberdeen, advertised the classes through the Workers' Educational Association and 70 women turned up. After that it mushroomed.

'It's very much about self-confidence and self-esteem', says Christine. 'Unless you feel you have a right to defend yourself, it's very difficult to do so. So it's about women's rights and awareness . . . I suppose it could be called consciousness-raising.'

> It's the coming together, sharing experiences, raising confidence with each other and plugging in to the fact that you're not the only one that certain things are happening to. But I don't think in a lot of communities if you put up a notice that you were going

to have a consciousness-raising class, that women would turn out to it ... Feminism can be a very frightening word, and a very misunderstood word ... It is something we talk about nearly immediately in the first of the sessions but we quite quickly de-mystify it and say simply that feminism is about choice and equality.

As with the other women's groups mentioned above, the self-defence network has never received proper funding. Ideally, her fantasy for Glasgow – and Scotland – would be that every community would have a women's centre, resourced with information, books, creche, library, a gym and self-defence classes. Or that buildings which are now under-used and often male-dominated, such as leisure centres and gyms, should have women-only days once or twice a week. Christine thinks that all funding bodies should see self-defence as something that should be provided for women.

Training in self-defence should also be available in schools, for both girls and boys. The material she uses could be adapted for work with children. She finds it interesting that in Scotland some assertive-ness work is already being done with pupils in schools, for example, in terms of child sexual abuse, drugs, alcohol and smoking.

There's quite a big movement going on to empower children and give them the techniques to say 'no' to a number of these issues. But I see that as a selective empowerment. We don't look at it holistically and say 'let's work with children in all areas and all issues from quite an early age'.

Christine regrets Scotland's disciplined and authoritarian-centred type of education. She would prefer a holistic, child-centred education system where all the issues are looked at together: 'We can't ask children to say "no" to drugs and alcohol but not say "no" to a teacher that's maybe thumped you right across the room.'

So far as male violence is concerned, children and women are breaking the silence, though the level is still unknown.

Some sources are bandying about for domestic violence and sexual abuse figures like one in four ... from my personal experience and by the women I work with, and in the last 10 years, I can only see it as endemic. I think the figures would be horrendous if we knew them truly. And I think if we truly wanted to know them we *could* know them. But I don't think

society wants to know them, or look at that horrifying side of life
. . . Sexual abuse, rape, assault, domestic violence, rape within
marriage, and male-to-male violence – the level is enormous. But
specifically looking at the violence to women and children, I
would say it's comparable to a war – it's genocide; it's
overwhelming.

Christine's early work with unemployed workers' centres, toddlers'
groups and play groups had made her suspect what was going on, but
she did not have any real evidence. Since 1983, when she started work
with Hamilton Women's Aid, all of these suspicions have been borne
out. She can see now that it is a global issue: getting women and
children to safety from violent men happens all over the world.
    Christine's work in the community has had a major effect on her
life.

In the last 10 years of my life there's been such personal growth
and such major changes for me, and the main reason has been
because the work that I do has led me to understand what
happened to me in my past life. It doesn't seem a very profound
thing to say, but it helped me make sense of my life, and that was
really powerful. And it didn't only help me then, it helps me now.

Her parents split up when she was 11 and, although she is not sure if
there was physical violence, there was certainly mental and emotional
abuse, and she struggled for years trying to make sense of why it
happened. She and her four sisters coped together with the traumas.
Her work with women and her 'coming to feminism' finally helped
her to deal with the past, 'to depower it and to empower me'. One of
the things she wants to communicate to women, if she can, is:

You can get strength and support. If you choose to take control
of your life – and control's a relative word in our society – you
can make sense of it, you can grow, and one of the very
rewarding things about working in Women's Aid – and there's a
lot of very distressing things – is that some women, some of the
time, do go through that process.

Sadly, for a lot of reasons – mainly economic – many women go
back to aggressive partners. The whole approach of Women's Aid is
to highlight options, and support the women, whatever choice they
make. But Women's Aid also believes in sharing knowledge and

information with the women, such as helping them to understand that violence is unacceptable, and that no one has a right to beat and abuse them.

Many, many women have never heard anybody say that to them. They quite clearly at times will tell you that it is their fault, because they didn't have the tea on the table at six o'clock, the boiled egg was too soft, or wee Jimmy was crying in the corner and therefore that deserved a broken nose.

The work has also helped her to discover her own identity beyond the roles society imposed on her.

Much of my life was very much as a daughter, a mother and a wife, in that order. I was pregnant when I was 16, had children very young, and I never really knew who I was, or what skills or contributions I could make. The last 10 years in this type of work were very powerful for me in that I now know people that know me as me rather than as a wife and a mother. As far as I can see from talking to other women, it's a very common process.

If you're going to be active in the community, according to Christine, you have to like people, and she really does – particularly women. She loves women's company, and children's. She also feels that she wants to make some kind of contribution back to the community, no matter how small. She thinks quite a lot of people feel like that, 'And that actually makes you feel good.'

Being involved with like-minded people, challenging something, and working towards it, you get so much out of it . . . for me it started with my younger son getting in to playgroup, and I had a couple of hours to spare each week. I did the usual things with my pals and sat drinking tea and coffee, and then I got bored and looked for things to do.

When Christine's children were older and she was able to go back to paid work, she got a job as a community work assistant. She then started to learn quite a lot about working with groups and trying to mobilise them. After two and a half years, she went to college to become qualified as a community worker. She thinks that you can motivate people to do something, but there are particular skills involved. Some of these you do not have to learn because they are about relating to people and liking them, and tuning in to what the issues are.

But how can you motivate people in impoverished communities who are struggling with basic issues, such as housing, heating, food and families?

One of the words I hate, and a lot of people use it a lot of the time, is apathy. They say people are apathetic or communities are apathetic. The fact is they're exhausted, they're struggling. How do you wake up every morning and survive day to day in some of the conditions that people are living in? It's really, really hard . . .

Schemes to help them are often imposed by politicians or councillors from the top down. 'They write a wee paper, get in there and do a wee bit and it's all hunky dory for a while. But back at the ranch nothing is actually happening, and the resources are just jobs for the boys.' She believes therefore that such schemes have to come from the bottom up, as then they have firmer foundations and are what people want. But, in her experience, that is not usually what happens. People's poverty gets manipulated.

Many people, and especially women, could be helped to become more active if, for instance, their fares were paid to meetings, or a creche were provided, or expenses for a creche were paid.

Christine believes that one of the most important things about community work is that it should be recorded – written down, photographed, or taperecorded. For, so often, the achievements of the working classes, women and/or people from the ethnic communities are rewritten or lost.

In Scotland, and under the last 10 years of Thatcher, it's been such a struggle that you have to keep writing down achievements and how far you've got, measured to the power you're up against. Because if you don't morale gets so low that you feel you're not getting anywhere. Primitive people painted pictures on walls of what they'd done and we have oral traditions of handing things down. We have to find ways of doing that again, because if we don't, it's disappearing, and if it disappears, that's dangerous.

CHAPTER 7

ELEANOR HOLMES

*There are people who can give and people who can't . . . I think it
is a giving thing . . . You have to be the sort of person who is
willing to give of themselves.*

Eleanor Holmes has made a profession out of being a volunteer. She
is the Manchester area organiser for the Women's Royal Voluntary
Service (WRVS) – an area with 10 metropolitan divisions and a total
of about 5,000 active volunteers. WRVS has its origins in the years
preceding the Second World War. In 1938 the Home Secretary, Sir
Samuel Hoare, asked the Dowager Marchioness of Reading to form
an organisation to help local authorities recruit women for the Air
Raid Precautions Services.

The new organisation gradually extended its work to feeding,
clothing and sheltering people during wartime emergencies and,
more recently, to providing various different services within the
community. Perhaps best known is the meals on wheels service which
was pioneered by the WRVS. Other duties carried out by the WRVS
include running hospital shops, providing holidays for children and
families in need, and providing clothing and bedding.

WRVS, which today has around 170,000 volunteers, still has an
emergency role and in most of the recent national disasters – such as
Lockerbie, the Clapham rail crash and the Hillsborough disaster –
WRVS volunteers, many of them in their green uniforms, are often
very much to the fore, providing food and comfort for the emergency
services and victims alike.

Eleanor started volunteering for WRVS in 1973 and has gradually
'risen through the ranks'. She had been trained as an ophthalmic
optician, but after having two children she felt unable to go back to a
full-time job.

If I had gone back I would have been working furiously to pay for a housekeeper to look after the family. I didn't want someone to bring up the children who didn't stimulate them and this is what you have to settle for sometimes. You are torn. Probably this is why we have quite a lot of volunteers. You want to do something, but you don't want it to interfere totally with your family.

Instead, she saw an advert in the local paper in Oldham for someone to do the trolley service around the wards. She started off doing the trolley duty once a week and then moved on to running the hospital shop. Shortly after, she became the metropolitan organiser for Oldham and began to spend more of her time as a volunteer.

When I took over it was a higher commitment. It started off as two to three days a week and it became three days a week. My commitment now is not a lot more than that, because I do other things with my life. I am a magistrate on the Oldham Bench which accounts for a day a fortnight, plus training. And my husband has always taken Friday off so I try to keep Fridays fairly clear. So now I'm here three days a week plus evening meetings and what have you, so it's quite controllable.

Although Eleanor sometimes regrets not going back to her profession, she now recognises that she has carved a different kind of career for herself in a way which has allowed her to preserve her commitments to her family. But what was it that made her choose the WRVS?

I was thinking about this. I was brought up in a village in Derbyshire and things only happen there if people do things voluntarily. I used to help with carnivals and cricket club teas and things like that. You get roped into things. My mother also used to do the distribution of welfare foods. She used to get her supplies from a village a few miles away so I often used to go with her to collect them. So it is a whole thing that develops. As a teenager I went off it all, but it was there in my background. And when my youngest daughter was starting school I was just about fed up with domestic work and so I was looking for something.

The Manchester area of WRVS is a large organisation. Its local offices organise meals on wheels, hospital shops, work with disabled and elderly people, and luncheon clubs. One new project just starting up is a centre for parents who have separated from their children to meet up in. 'It's much better than McDonalds', says Eleanor. At the centre of this enormous hub of activity, it is Eleanor's job to ensure that everything works. 'Basically, it is getting the volunteers out to do a job in the community.' But the meals on wheels service alone can be an enormous undertaking.

The mere taking out of a round of meals on wheels is far more than two people turning up to do it every day. In this area, we have several projects where we cook and go right through to delivery. We have to handle quite a lot of money and account for it. The turnover in any one district is quite amazing. With the hospital shops, we are no longer talking about a small business. The turnover is running into millions. Turnover in the other projects in Manchester is around half a million pounds.

There are also all the vehicles to keep on the road, rotas to be filled, negotiations with local authorities and other caring organisations and dozens of other tasks. For the first time, WRVS has now had to consider conducting management training for its volunteers. Despite this, there are still large numbers of people who are willing to do the work, almost all of it given entirely free.

We have a very small bit of help with secretarial work and we do pay what are very small grants to enable people to do the job. In quite a few instances, we have single parents or widowed people who are limited in what they can earn and are quite happy with a modest grant to help them out. We also pay out-of-pocket expenses. That is very necessary these days. You can't expect them to do voluntary work and pay for it as well. That doesn't fit into the modern ways. For someone working in one of the shops for five days a week, with all the responsibility, I think we have to recognise that – not in a salary as such, but in terms of a small grant.

WRVS has always had an image of being run by middle-aged, middle-class women, but Eleanor refutes this.

Sociologically they are completely mixed – in age, aspirations and every other way. The old image may be a bit truer in the counties, but not here. The tendency is for us to have more volunteers in the early-retired bracket, but we have them right through from young people doing their Duke of Edinburgh's badges, and so on. Obviously, we miss out on the middle years because those are the family and career years generally. Having said that, we have some evening projects where people who work full-time can help.

Once they have started working for WRVS, people (10 per cent of the membership is actually made up of men!) tend to stay around. The exceptions, says Eleanor, are the unemployed people who come to them. Many of these come to get themselves a bit of confidence so that they can feel better about applying for jobs. 'It's lovely to see them get a job', she says. 'It's one of the nice bits of the work.'

At the same time, the confidence-building side of working with WRVS can have some unintended effects.

We lose quite a lot of volunteers because for somebody who has had an ordinary upbringing, brought up a family and then comes to us, they develop confidence and suddenly the husbands see their little lady asserting herself, and that doesn't always go down well. I had had a career so, in a way, that was a slight difference. But when I started doing something, I found I lacked confidence dreadfully. If you have never had that because you had lived a very ordinary life, then it must be even harder. We are very aware of that and recognise that a lot of people need plenty of support when they first come to us.

She gives the example of one of the Manchester metropolitan organisers who, when she first started volunteering five years ago, was 'like a mouse'. 'She has developed so beautifully, it is lovely to see. She has really come on. Sometimes you wonder if people can do anything. The ones that seem to be best in the first instance often fade, while the ones that just creep in come along well, especially with a bit of nurturing.'

The national emergency aspect of WRVS is now only a small part of the organisation. But it still responds to disasters, providing support to the main rescue services.

At Lockerbie, we were providing meals for four weeks. And those poor lads who were finding all sorts of awful things – they were coming in for meals and they needed to talk. And we were talked at for want of a better expression. It was a by-product of what we were supposed to be doing, but it was vital.

After the Manchester air crash – in which an airliner burst into flames on the runway and nearly 60 people died – WRVS was involved in the hospitals, and taking families to visit relatives as well as providing refreshment and talking to people. There is a county emergency service which calls out the back-up services. It has only happened once to Eleanor, when she was the Oldham metropolitan organiser.

It was seven o'clock one Sunday morning and I was fast asleep. Someone had ripped a gas meter off the wall in a block of flats and they had to evacuate the flats and they needed somebody to go down and cope with refreshments in a nearby school. We had a car with equipment there in 20 minutes. I alerted the local organiser and she passed the message on and, while she was doing that, I was thinking about how to get the cooks there. These are the kinds of things that go through your head. As WRVS organiser, your job is to get people there, not necessarily to go yourself. You are the contact point and you shouldn't leave your post. In actual fact, I am second on the list here because we have one lady who doesn't drive and it's far easier for her to act as the centre while we get things moving.

In a more complex and technically advanced world, is there still a role for an amateur emergency service, or even for a voluntary meals on wheels service? Will changes to care in the community make it difficult for people to continue doing voluntary work, knowing that others may perhaps be receiving a wage for doing exactly the same kind of work? Eleanor does not think so. It is perhaps more difficult to find the senior organisers because that requires more commitment. They are supposed to be self-replacing and this is not usually a problem, although it was before they brought in compulsory retirement at 65. Before that people tended to go on too long and delay finding a replacement.

One of our biggest problems is organisers who retire when their only interest in life is WRVS. It can be a very bitter end because they feel they have given their life and then suddenly it ends. But if you don't retire, there is no continuity. We have been able to do that here, but we have to be very careful. The lady who I replaced is now working in the baby shop at Hope Hospital. She always wanted to do hospital work, but never had the time when she was area organiser.

She thinks that people will continue to volunteer and that WRVS will carry on its work. It will require greater appreciation of management skills to assess what people are capable of and how they can be encouraged. 'Those people who come along and say they can do several days a week are usually the ones who fall flat on their faces', says Eleanor. 'The ones who start by saying they can do one day a week or fortnight often come along nicely. And I think it is a good thing, because you need to find out if you like the work before you go headlong into it.'

Volunteering for Eleanor is, she says, linked to personality. 'There are people who can give and people who can't. I think it is a giving thing, without wishing to be pompous. You have to be the sort of person who is willing to give of themselves.'

In terms of citizenship, she sees volunteering as part of the process of building inner strength and confidence.

It follows on from things like guides and scouts and Duke of Edinburgh's, and so on. That is probably where tomorrow's volunteers will come from – people who have done that sort of thing. Because it is a service to the community. You get out of voluntary work as much as you put in. Nice things happen sometimes, like the organiser I mentioned who developed her strength and confidence.

Eleanor also talks of the memorable experiences she has had which have come through her voluntary work – being presented to the Queen Mother and to the Princess Royal, and a garden party at Buckingham Palace: 'I know these things matter more to some people than to others, but I would never have got within miles of these things if I hadn't done the work.' She also puts down her appointment as a magistrate to her voluntary work. 'It didn't come directly from my WRVS work, but that was part of the reason. It came from being part of the community and being known.'

Another of her interests which has come from doing voluntary work is her membership of Soroptimist International: 'I mix with other people from all over the country and that is worth a lot to me because it really broadens your interests. And that is something I would never have got if I had returned to work.'

One of the things about this job is that wherever you go in the country you can meet a group of people of like mind. And that helps you in your work because it is quite a hard job and, if there wasn't this support, it would be very much harder. What does active citizenship mean to me? I suppose it is basically what I am doing. Some people said when I got married and gave up my job that I was 'throwing it all away', but I think it really shows there is another way. I'd like to think that any loss to society had been more than made up for by the things I do today.

CHAPTER 8

MARGY WOODWARD

It means gaining confidence and saying how you would like your life to be led . . . this is why I am now totally emotionally involved, because I think there is so much to be done.

Margy Woodward has led a varied life – dog trainer and breeder, pet shop owner, bartender and, most recently, a volunteer visiting schools to talk to pupils about her disability, cerebral palsy. Now aged 35, she has always lived independently. Despite some lack of control over her body movements and speech, her enthusiasm and sense of fun are infectious.

One of my earliest memories is going to Great Ormond Street with these great heavy leg things on – very frightening. I don't remember much about it except the physiotherapy. I can pick up anything with my feet which is quite useful – saves you bending down when you've got no shoes on.

Margy went to a private primary school for able-bodied children, passed her ll-plus and, as her family had money at that time, was put down to go to the exclusive Benenden School. 'In fact, I would have been there with Princess Anne, but that's another story. Benenden at that time didn't think it was appropriate that they should have disabled people. They said they didn't think I could cope.'

Instead, she went to Lord Mayor Treloar's School, a specialist school for people with disabilities who had average or above-average intelligence.

It was actually the first time I had run into people with disabilities and it was terrifying, a tremendous jolt to the system. I had always been sheltered in a way, but going to Treloar did me a hell of a lot of good. It taught me there were people who were worse off, people who could do things, people who couldn't.

Margy did not do as well at school as she had wanted to, partly because of family problems, but her first ambition on leaving at 16 was to get a car. 'I found this noddy car and applied for a licence. What should I put down on the bit where it says "any disabilities"? CP or spastic or what? In the end I settled on "lack of muscular co-ordination". Anyway, I got it.'

Her first job in a supermarket checkout lasted four days until someone asked her to work quicker. She left and started working as a volunteer with guide dogs for the blind. 'They didn't pay me, but I did the same work as everyone else. I thought it would be good training for when I could have my own kennels.' Margy stayed for four years and then applied to go to Hereward College in Coventry to study book-keeping.

Hereward is a college for disabled people. 'I had the best year of my life there because I worked during the day and played like hell during the night. It was there that I became aware how much more I had attained than other people with disabilities and I also met the other type of disabled person – people from the army and navy who had had accidents.'

She left a year later and bought a kennels near Southampton, starting a breeding programme with labradors. For the next six years it was all hard work, with five staff under her. The kennels held up to 100 dogs and 10 cats on a five-acre spread. But after getting into financial problems and still only 25, Margy decided to sell the business. 'I basically retired for four years. I kept on showing and breeding dogs, but for myself.' She still has two pugs which go everywhere with her.

Living in the heart of the New Forest, Margy was keeping 14 labradors, showing and breeding them. Then she began to experience health problems: 'My back began to go. The wear and tear of CP accelerates the disintegration. I was also a bit of a buffoon, walking 10 or 15 miles a day, all over the forest. It takes its toll. I was told to lay off and find something else.'

This turned out to be a pet shop in Highcliffe in Hampshire. She says that it taught her tolerance and that some people could have an adverse reaction to her physical appearance. So life was shared with jerbils and rabbits, parrots and mynah birds: 'I could never really deal with the birds because they take one look at me and freak out.'

The pet shop, too, did not really work out and Margy once again

sold out. With no commitments and little to occupy herself, she was
saved from despondency and self-pity by the landlady of a local pub
who asked her to come in and work in the bar. 'As a natural buffoon I
loved it. I used to do the cash & carry, banking, go to the brewery, in
fact everything. I worked there solid doing eight sessions a week.'
    In fact, although Margy enjoyed the work and became a firm
favourite with many of the pub's regulars, she was still not happy.
Then, quite by chance, her sister-in-law fixed her up with an
appointment with someone from the Spastics Society. 'For God's
sake, what do you think I am,' I told her when I found out. 'But then I
thought it might be worth going along. I hadn't dealt with them for all
these years.' Some weeks later she was interviewed by the Society.

> The interview covered dexterity, intelligence and everything else.
> One of the questions was 'what is the connection between a fly
> and a tree?' I still don't know the answer to that one. But they
> asked me if I wanted to go on an alternative life-styles course. I'd
> lived all my life on my own. I've always been independent. If it's
> about learning to peel potatoes, I thought, you can get stuffed.
> In fact, I picked out sailing, skiing and computer work.

Margy found herself in a new kind of environment, bombarded
with information and tested in ways she had never been before.
Because she had been so independent and had come from a
comparatively wealthy background, she says that it had never come
home to her that there were many disabled people who were literally
striving to get out of the front door, let alone doing their own thing.
'It was a great awakening for me', she says.
    After the course, she was asked if she would consider showing a
film in schools about cerebral palsy. 'It's called *The Land of Droog*
and it raises many of the issues of disability.' Margy had been
working in the pub for about two years at this stage and did not quite
know what to do. In the end, she went along to the local Spastics
Society office in Portsmouth and was given another formal interview.

> I think I passed because we went out that afternoon to visit five
> schools. They showed me where they were on the *A–Z* and told
> me to get on with it. That was in March 1989 and I have not
> stopped since then. On average, I do four schools, colleges or
> groups of social workers a week.

Margy has since been back on the life-styles course, but as a tutor.

She has gained confidence and has made talking to school children into a speciality.

> The schools I go into, the message is quite dramatic. For the 11-to 12-year-olds I walk into an assembly and say, 'Right, the first thing you know about me is that I wobble a bit, I jerk a bit and my speech is a bit defective. This is not because I have been in the pub all day . . .' That usually puts them at their ease. And then I say, 'How many of you have called someone an old spazzo or a spastic? Well it's not very funny when you meet someone like me. It's not to be ridiculed. It's called cerebral palsy, but we will call it CP for short.' And then you show the video.

Margy says that the message she tries to get across is that disability is much more common than we like to admit. One person in seven has a disability and really everyone has one of some kind because none of us can do everything. 'We talk about sporting handicaps and I try to get them to see that disability is as much about attitude as anything else.'

She has found the experience of talking to young people has its own rewards:

> When they see this strange person wobbling round the place they are a bit put off, but once you begin to speak and they see you've got an intelligent mind they will give you their all – they really do. I go into rough Portsmouth and Southampton schools where before I would have been terrified to go. And after I've done my speech the kids come up to me and say, 'I couldn't stand up there and do that miss. How do you do it?' I want them to understand that we are not different, nobody's different. If you could only accept colour, religion, and so on, you wouldn't have half the wars and trouble that we've got. Disability is an easy way of understanding this.

The decision to become involved in work with the Spastics Society and schools has made Margy reassess her own life and her attitude to other people with CP. She has become interested in self-advocacy and is now active within a small ginger group of people with CP within the Society called Alpha. She sees two roles for herself as an articulate and confident person with CP:

> We've got to convince the 'normal' people that we are not freaks

and then we've also got to go to people like ourselves and say, 'You can do it, people aren't going to laugh at you.' This is what we do through Alpha – self-advocacy. It means gaining confidence and saying how you would like your life to be led, not how other people have told you how your life ought to be led. This is why I am now emotionally totally involved, because I think there is so much to be done. And prior to a year ago, I hadn't a clue what was going on.

Margy says that people such as herself are seen as the under-privileged and are treated as such by society. If people do not know how to cope with disabled people they back off, because they are frightened of the unknown.

We have to show them that we aren't freaks and that we have a right to be heard and not just patted on the head. Some disabilities are appalling – many people with brittle bone disease, for example, often have the most grotesque freatures, but I have a friend from Treloar who is now an architectural development officer for disabled people. She is brittle boned and people see her and can't handle it – until she gets her message across and they begin to relate to her as a human being.

Attitudes to disability are changing, Margy believes, but she still comes across people who try to make fun at her expense, although now she normally has the last word.

A few weeks ago I had these kids following me along the pavement in Bournemouth. You know, as you go past these shops with the big windows I could see them mimicking how I was walking. So I let them catch up with me and then I said, 'Look, if you want to take the piss, do it properly. You're not throwing your left leg out far enough.' They were terribly embarrassed. Maybe that's a bit mean on my part, but those kids will never do it again to anybody else.

CHAPTER 9

COLIN LOW

*I have had quite a lot of advantages in life . . . and I think I owe it
to try and put something back. There is a bit more. If I'm honest,
I enjoy it.*

Colin Low was born with defective sight – congenital glaucoma. He
was not completely blind and in the first few years of his life he had a
series of operations to try and improve his sight. But the last vestiges
of vision were lost when, aged three, he ran into a cupboard door at
his nursery school. From then on, he was brought up and educated as
a blind person.

> I deal with the whole of life as a blind person. People argue about
> whether or not it is better to lose one's sight at birth or later on.
> They usually vote for their own circumstances. For myself, I'm
> glad not to have had a loss of sight to adjust to, having been in a
> condition where total blindness was always a taken-for-granted
> aspect of the world which you didn't have to get used to.

Colin's blindness has not stopped him involving himself in a wide
range of organisations and activities, particularly those promoting
the interests of blind people. At 47, he now heads the London
Boroughs Disability Resource Team which provides disability advice
and services for 10 London boroughs.

The present team was salvaged from the wreckage of the Greater
London Council (GLC) after it was abolished in 1986. Before that, it
had been the GLC's Disability Unit. Despite being active on
disablement throughout his adult life, this is the first job Colin has
held professionally which deals with issues of disability.

Although his family is in Leeds and he returns there every weekend,
he has lived and worked in London for the past five years. This in
itself has been an important experience: 'The first three years in

London I stayed as a lodger. But for the last two years I've been living on my own and, for the first time in my life, I've become much more self-sufficient.'

More than anything else, Colin has spent much of his time campaigning and working on issues to do with the education of blind people. He was asked to join a committee set up by the National Innovation Centre (which was founded by Michael Young) and helped to produce a report on the provision for disabled students in higher education.

After that, Lord Snowdon set up a committee on integrating disabled people, serviced by the charity Action Research for the Crippled Child ('not a title anyone would use now if they were setting up an organisation', he says), and Colin was asked to join the committee.

> It was a huge committee of about 40 people. I was on two of the subcommittees – one on employment and the other on education. Someone else was due to chair the latter, but they backed out and I became chair. That really started me off and it's grown from there.

His work on education has included lobbying around the Education Act 1981 and work with the Advisory Centre for Education on the subject of integrating children with special needs into mainstream education. In 1975 he joined the council of the Royal National Institute for the Blind (RN1B) and, shortly after, its education committee, becoming its vice chairman in 1982 and chairman in 1984.

He also worked with the National Bureau for Handicapped Students (since renamed the National Bureau for Students with Disabilities). He was on the steering committee that set it up and was vice chairman for five years, eventually bowing out in 1981.

Colin himself, from the age of three, always went to separate schools for blind people.

> I lived in a small town just outside Edinburgh. Rather against my mother's better judgement, I was sent away to the nursery department of a blind school as soon as possible. I was sent away on a weekly basis. I didn't like it very much and was very unhappy. I think that, for a long time, I repressed the memory of that, but it came back in later life and I think it would be true to say that that has constituted a scar.

Soon after, he was sent away to a Sunshine Home in England, an infant school run by the RNIB. From the age of five to seven he boarded away from home, but returned to Scotland for his primary education. Then once again, aged 11, he was sent away to Worcester in England to a boarding school run by the RNIB.

It was really for children of grammar school ability. I got a good traditional education there. I was quite happy. Of course, socially it was restricted. They didn't teach you as much about life skills then as they do now. I was aware that there was an argument about whether to educate blind people along with sighted people, but we never had that argument at school.

It was only later, after a degree at Oxford, a postgraduate diploma at Cambridge, further postgraduate work at Oxford and then a teaching job at Leeds University that the arguments about education began to take form. Although he graduated in law, he moved over into criminology and then into law and sociology, which he taught at Leeds University for 16 years from 1968.

At Leeds, Colin began to get active in a small way with the National Federation of the Blind. He became associated with another blind colleague who had been to a unique school for both blind and sighted children in Glasgow during the thirties and forties.

I came under his influence and worked with him and we had rather an exciting time in the Federation at the beginning of the seventies when we were developing its policies. We did a lot in terms of developing the policy in the Federation in a principled and philosophical way. One of the principles we developed was that of integration.

At that time there was no official acceptance of the arguments in favour of integration. Although Colin's Worcester school had been integrated when it was first established 100 years ago, that had quickly been abandoned. The Royal Commonwealth Society for the Blind had always promoted joint learning; this was mainly for cost reasons. In the Federation and the RNIB there were strong currents of opinion in favour of separate education.

After much lobbying and campaigning, support for integration was eventually won in the Federation by a majority of two to one.

Rather strikingly, at the beginning of the seventies, education was the most contentious issue at the Federation's meetings, but since the policy was agreed, it is the one issue that never features from year to year. No motions or questions have been raised over the last six or seven years.

Colin admits that, although the battle has been won in the Federation, it has not been won in the wider world. British society, he says, is more segregated in its approach to education than many other countries. For example, in Scandinavia, and the United States education for blind people is almost entirely integrationist. Northern European countries – Germany, France and Britain – have a strong bias towards special schooling.

But things are changing. The RNIB runs a number of segregated schools, but it also now puts resources into local authorities to help them do more for blind children in integrated schools. Up to now, this has had more impact on the education of partially sighted children.

I'm implicated in a major way because I'm chairman of the RNIB's education committee and although there has been investment in the school in Worcester, for example, to bring it up to date as opposed to close it and transfer the resources, it was just one of those battles which I lost. You might say why did I stay on as chairman, but there are other things one can do as well.

Besides involving himself fully in the continuing debate about education, Colin has always been a firm advocate of blind people playing a major role in the organisations for the blind. As already mentioned, much of his voluntary work has been with the National Federation of the Blind, a small organisation with just over 1,000 supporters and run on a voluntary basis. He contrasts it with the RNIB which he sees as a 'for' organisation, not controlled by blind people. By 1989, 56 of the 96 members of RNIB's executive were visually handicapped but, of them, only 30 actually represented blind people's organisations. The rest were individuals. The majority of RNIB's paid employees, including its director general, were sighted; 8 per cent of staff were visually handicapped.

Having said that, things have changed. We had a big campaign to open up the RNIB to make it more accountable. When we started, it had an executive council of 120, of whom only eight were blind. Shortly before that it had been two. The RNIB had a review and offered another four places for blind people. We managed to jack it up to 30 and that made a big difference. But even now it is still only a third.

But, says Colin, it is not just a question of quantity. The blind people are very active and possibly exert a disproportionate influence.

We have made a big impact since that first change in 1975. The representative ones of us now occupy the leading chairmanships of the main standing committees. The matter is under review and the RNIB is now looking at its constitution again. It has accepted the principle of moving towards 50 per cent.

Colin feels that there is no point in simply employing staff because they are blind.

Aspects of experience that a blind person has access to are not available to a sighted person. But having said that, there are a lot of sighted people that I would gladly have working for blind people. It is possible for sighted people to have skills that some blind people do not have. A sighted person might have considerable research and analytical skills and a blind person might be able to identify closely with other blind people, so both are needed.

As he became more involved with the National Federation of the Blind, Colin was, in turn, public relations officer, general secretary, vice president and president. He has been on the executive continuously since 1969. He was also in the Disablement Income Group (DIG) between 1972 and 1974, but left to join the Disability Alliance when it was formed in 1974 with the aim of bringing together everyone who wanted a better income for disabled people. He has been on the Disability Alliance committee continuously since 1980 and has been vice chair since 1988.

What motivates him to spend so much of his time working on a voluntary basis for so many organisations?

I can't really think of anything besides something rather corny really. I think I have had quite a lot of advantages in life. I had a good education which has enabled me to get good jobs and so on, and I think I owe it to try and put something back.

There is a bit more. If I'm honest, I enjoy it. I enjoy
the politicking that's associated with it. I enjoy the kind of
work.

Are blind people generally – and other people with disabilities –
more concerned about citizenship and representation, and does the
concept of empowering mean more to them than to society at large?
Colin believes that it is a minority of both blind and sighted people
who are interested in changing and doing things, as opposed to being
passive.

I think a lot of people in the blind world, at some inarticulate
level, are conscious of something being wrong, of them being
one down, or not properly regarded or listened to, or given a fair
deal. Another way of saying that is to call it disempowerment. At
some level, people are aware of that, but not so aware of doing
something about it.

But he adds that amongst the minority of active blind people is a
mature, responsible, coherent group. 'The kind of stance they have
taken about their condition is a very balanced and sane and sober
one.' It is, he says, more balanced than the consciousness of the
disabled movement in general.

The orthodoxy that disabled people are increasingly articulating
is that disability isn't a problem. If it is a problem, it is one of
society's making. It is society that puts the handicap into
disability. Apostles of the disabled movement react against
notions like 'problem' and of 'helping' people. I think society is
beginning to buy these arguments and, in fact, I think they are
rather distorted. The non-disabled world tends to accept them
because they are inhibited about challenging what a disabled
person says about their condition.

Colin refers to these views as a kind of heresy. 'Blind people, on the
other hand, hold that blindness is a serious disadvantage and a
handicap, and you don't do them any kind of favour by glossing over
that, or ignoring it, or pretending that they are not blind and treating
them as if they were sighted.'
He agrees that society has wrongly stressed the 'problem' nature of
disability and that the problem lies with the individual and that, in
most cases, it is a medical issue.

That is all wrong, but it is equally wrong to say that it is entirely the other way round and that disabled people are not different in any way at all. We have to stress both. Professionals have definitely overstressed the medical approach and now disabled activists tend to overstress the social model, as it is called. I strongly believe that it is not either/or, but one needs to fuse both perspectives.

Nonetheless, he accepts that society is becoming more open to ideas about blind people's abilities. Colin says that the number of people who think that, if you want to do something about blindness, you have to talk to blind people is increasing.

In the past they would just have pushed ahead. Within RNIB and other organisations there is much more of an awareness that you cannot do this in the way it was done in the past. Whether you involve them in quite the right way can be open to argument. But it would be unthinkable without involving blind people.

CHAPTER 10

DAVID WRAGG

We know that if we can get people to work for us, they come back again and again and again – because we can offer them a smashing day out.

David Wragg was a cheese broker in his own dairy business until he was forcibly bought out at the age of 50 in 1985. Shortly after, he became Director of the Leicestershire and Rutland Trust for Nature Conservation: 'They wanted a salesman who could go to anybody and everybody and instead of selling cheese sell the environment.'

His post was one-third funded by the Nature Conservancy Council for the first three years, 'to get the show on the road'. But they have paid the price of success and, in addition to fundraising for the Trust, he now has to raise his own salary – a major task even though it's barely one-third of what he was earning in his own business.

The Trust, formed 32 years ago, now has 40 nature reserves which include some very important and unique sites, such as Rutland Water which is leased from Anglian Water. It owns about 2,500 acres and manages the same amount again. Like 47 other wildlife trusts nationally (which have a total membership of 204,000), it is affiliated to the Royal Society for Nature Conservation (RSNC) and is, like them, according to the RSNC's Annual Report, 'autonomous, locally owned and run by active citizens'.

David's job certainly requires a lot of action. As director, with just one full-time conservation officer and part-time secretarial help, he is responsible for fundraising, marketing, publicity, managing the reserves (including farming them, if appropriate), and ensuring a supply of volunteers. 'We are clever managers', he says. 'We manage to keep going and show a profit each year and, at the same time, achieve what we want.'

He takes a very pragmatic view of his role, and feels that in the old days the Trust was 'pretty elitist':

They bought land and put a fence round it and said 'Keep out of here' . . . But it's a heritage not just for the people who are here now. It's in trust for everyone, isn't it? I believe there's got to be new thinking. We've got to get nature reserves and say to people 'Will you come in? Don't go on that bit there because that's important, but you can come in and enjoy the rest of it.' If you get the community in, participating, then the community don't mind paying.

He was born at Oadby in Leicestershire and, as a youngster, was 'always aware of the country'. He became a technical dyer and finisher by trade, and joined the Trust 20 years ago because he was interested in 'going and looking at things, always a very keen birdwatcher'. Then he got involved in the committee of a small reserve near Market Harborough where he had business connections. 'I've always been a bit vociferous, at the forefront of supporting the Trust as a member.'

He believes that the Trust now is 'offering a hell of a facility, not just to our members (in 1989 around 4,500) but a country-wide facility'. Not only is it increasing the reserves all the time, but it is also trying to educate and inform people about what is going on, particularly that it is their environment that is under threat. 'In the twentieth century we've got to be realistic and have an approach that's acceptable to anybody.'

But his pragmatism is tinged with cynicism: 'Although people have got this concern, it's only a very small percentage who are really doing anything about it. It's a hell of a hard sell. What am I selling, really? Hope – an intangible, with no second-hand value to it.'

But he thinks it is better to preach hope and the responsibility to future generations rather than the threat. This approach enables him to identify businesses that are looked on as major, or minor, pollutants and talk to them to see if they can work together.

I say to my council and to my contemporaries, 'Look, let's not be anti everything for the sake of being anti, let's get the best we can out of them and talk to the planners, the builders, the tree-fellers beforehand and see what we can save, what we can create . . . and the developers and builders now come to me and say 'There's plans for a massive greenfield site [previously two golf courses]: are you going to try and stop it?' We only object on scientific grounds, if it's a Site of Special Scientific Interest. But I certainly make suggestions: 'Don't fill in the ponds, leave them as a feature'; 'Plant as many trees as you like', and 'If you're planting a golf course make sure you're not hitting golf balls into any of the woodland.'

But he finds that he is rarely preaching to the converted, even now. Although the membership is growing slowly, it does not reflect the massive popular interest in the environment which chooses to support Friends of the Earth and Greenpeace: 'I'm always a little bit conscious of the nanny syndrome . . . if somebody's doing it, it's all right. This is one of the reasons I'm not sure if I'd like to see nature conservation taken over by local government, or by central government.'

A good example of this attitude is the public response to the City Wildlife Project, a scheme funded until 1989 by the Inner Area Programme of the Department of the Environment. At its height, this employed hundreds of young people in the Community Programme, who went into schools, created city nature areas, and made a comprehensive assessment of the environmental value of the city.

Because of its educational approach and good public relations it achieved a very high public profile. But the Trust's membership dropped. He asked people why this had happened. 'Oh, it's been done now, there's no need', they replied.

Others, he feels, are not active because they do not know there is a problem. One of the areas he feels has been neglected in the last 30 years is telling people what is going on. This is all tied up with money. If he had a big-enough publicity budget he thinks that he could treble the Trust's membership overnight. But over the last 10 years, the emphasis has been on protecting the nature reserves, rather than involving people.

So David feels that it is not surprising if people are unaware of what is happening and are not involved. The Trust took a poll near their office in Leicester when they launched a new Wildlife Appeal and found that less than 5 per cent had ever heard of them. This was after they had distributed 200,000 leaflets, advertised in the press, and David Attenborough had publicised the appeal by appearing on television, at their launch, and at a reserve two weeks later. They got full national coverage.

Even the people who had heard of them were not sure what they did. Did they look after cats . . . ? So his main priority is to keep telling people: 'If you don't yell, you don't sell.' There are always people becoming active, wanting to do something, but 'it's a slowly slowly job'. He believes that if they were to use lists, targetting certain people in Leicestershire, it would be people with names like Edith, Harry and Mavis, that sort of age group. They are always in desperate need of volunteers to work at the reserves:

> We know that if we can get people to work for us, they come back again and again and again – because we can offer them a smashing day out. If you're a big macho man you can go and whack a few trees down for a few days; if you're interested in basic recording of natural history, you can go and do it; if you're interested in walking you can go and do it. There's a variety of nice things – we're nice people, we're goodies. And we know that once we get people on our reserve committees – well, they die before they move away.

He thinks that people go through phases of being active citizens:

> The kids from 7 to 13 or 14 are very interested, very clever, very constructive, and you think you've got 'em. Then they suddenly discover boys – or girls – and for the next five years they couldn't care less one way or t'other. Then they've got to start thinking about a career, and higher education, and it's very difficult to commit yourself to a hobby as well.

David is unhappy about certain aspects of the green movement:

> One of the things that disturbs me at the moment is that there is a cynicism about the green initiative – a political cynicism and a commercial cynicism. It's 'Get on the bandwagon mate, there's money to be made here; get on the bandwagon, there's people to vote for you here.'

The only way to get through to people is to just continue to get your message over truthfully. He fervently believes that some conservation campaigns go a bit too far. As a classic example of this, he gives foxhunting, which causes a lot of bother. He personally is passionately against it, but the Trust is not. Some of its reserves were only given to it on the condition that hunting continued, so it allows hunting on most of its reserves on certain conditions. And he is against the protest activities which result 'because people identify the protest as some sort of hooliganism, where they should be identifying foxhunting as some sort of hooliganism. I'd rather talk to the hunt.' As a result, he and the hunters have built up a modus vivendi. If they hunt on Trust land they behave properly, otherwise they know they will be stopped. 'Now, would you believe, some members of the Cottesmore are as concerned about some aspects of nature conservation as my other members are.'

The Trust currently faces many problems. There is a grave shortage of funds and staff to carry out administration and reserve management, to implement its education policy, and to achieve the communication with the public which is necessary if it is to maintain and increase its membership. The government's Community Programme which, according to the Trust's annual report, provided 'endless manhours for three golden years towards managing our reserves, helping in our office and preparing our newsletter,' has now come to an end.

It is nervously facing water privatisation and its effects on Rutland Water Nature Reserve. Anglian Water refused to discuss the future of the reserves and their lease to the Trust until the Water Bill was passed. So all the Trust has been able to do is to urge its members to buy shares, so that they can have at least some influence on the final decision as to who will get the lease.

In trying to get the conservation message over, David has always tried to present a 'balanced, even message'. He is trying to get sponsorship from commercial sources – motor companies, construction companies, and others with a vested interest in the environment – and he feels he's beginning to make headway.

I'm a winner. I've been in business and I don't like losing. I believe we're making a very very important contribution to the next two to three generations. I'm not an alarmist. I don't like to say it's all too late, the world's collapsing, natural history's dying. I think with a little co-operation and a little bit of work we can get to a base from which we can progress. We can start planting trees instead of chopping them down.

CHAPTER 11

KATH CRIPPS

I am one of those people who has a conscience, and therefore can't sit back and just let things happen around me . . . I see injustice in so many different areas.

Kath Cripps, 53, peace campaigner and former JP, mother of four and grandmother of seven, has chosen to live on her own for the first time in her life in a small, spotless, terraced stone house in Hillsborough, a suburb of Sheffield.

On the wall in the kitchen is a poster with a quote by Peter Ustinov: 'I have never been stopped in the street by people collecting funds for nuclear weapons. Because this has been well taken care of by governments. But I have seen many collections for children.'

Kath says she is

one of those people who has a conscience, and therefore can't sit back and just let things happen around me. I sometimes wish I could, because I find myself getting involved in too many things because I see injustice in so many different areas. I'm a very active member of CND, I work full-time, and there are all kinds of issues attached to working for the Health Service (she is an occupational therapy helper at Sheffield Hospital). I'm still a member of the Labour Party, though slightly disillusioned at the minute, mostly because of the unilateral policy. I'm a union member. But, in a lot of ways, my activity is talking to people. I'm a great believer in talking to people over a cup of tea in a very ordinary manner and actually managing to put over points of what I believe . . . I'm a socialist and I like to point out socialist ideas, which are a part of ordinary life, after all.

She has recently been appointed on to the women's advisory committee of the Yorkshire and Humberside division of the National

Union of Public Employees (NUPE), but finds it very frustrating because advisory committees have no power. They have 'all these wonderful ideas when we meet together as a group of women and everything has to go through the next stage up which is composed mostly of men, and everything gets blocked.'

Whatever she has been involved in, she has always done one hundred per cent. She used to be a very keen member of the church, involved in Sunday school and Young Wives. But, as she got more involved politically, she found that the people in her church could not agree with her, especially on breaking the law. So she drifted away and never went back because 'although they talk about freedom within the church, until I came out of it I didn't really know what freedom was'.

She joined the Campaign for Nuclear Disarmament (CND) and became actively involved after her first granddaughter was born because she began to think about what the future would be like for the child. Kath did not like what was happening, and wanted her to have a future. This became a very important issue to her – some might say it took over her life – and she began going on CND demonstrations and doing everything possible to keep the group's head above water in Hathersage, Derbyshire, the area where she then lived, which was strongly Tory.

It was probably inevitable that her peace campaigning would, at some point, conflict with the other important voluntary activity in her life at that time – being a magistrate. Deciding to go on the bench had not been easy: 'You either accept the system we've got, and you're part of it, or you leave it to the Tories.'

Her decision to do so arose from attending a village meeting where there was a panel made up of people from various social services. She and her husband had recently fostered a boy who had been battered, and one of the questions asked of the panel was what they would do to the parents who had battered a child. One of the members of the panel, who was a magistrate,

> sat back on his chair with his thumbs in his braces – I can see him to this day – and would have strung her up, the mother. And I was so appalled, because I'd taken this child in, but no way would I have done anything like that to his mother. As far as I was concerned, whatever she was like there was a problem, and she needed help as much as he did. And I said to myself that day, if I ever get the opportunity I'll go on the bench, because that bloke isn't fit to be on there, and that was the start of it.

She was nominated from the Labour Party about a year later: 'I must have been a gift from the gods to them really, when I first went on, a working-class woman from the Labour Party', and was allocated to Bakewell Court in 1981, one of about 30 magistrates in the area.

Then, in mid-1984 a friend of hers, Margaret Roberts, at 72 faced a prison sentence for refusing to pay a £25 fine for obstructing an army lorry at Greenham Common Cruise missile base. The trial was scheduled to take place at her court at Bakewell, and her local CND group decided to mount a demonstration of support outside.

Kath looked at the rota to see if she was sitting and she was not. So she decided to join the local campaigners and stood outside the court holding a placard: 'Say no to illegal state policy'. She thought that she was within her rights as an individual to take this action, and was not aware and still does not accept that it is against the rules that govern being a magistrate.

She thinks that if she had joined such a protest in Sheffield it would have passed unnoticed. However, she was spotted by a local reporter and because it was in rural West Derbyshire the incident hit the headlines – 'Peace Demo Magistrate Faces Rap'; 'JP Faces Sack for Court Demo'.

She was summoned to an interview with the Lord Lieutenant of the county, and he issued an ultimatum asking her to promise never to take part in a demonstration outside any court ever again. She refused to make that promise, believing that it would infringe her democratic rights, and he asked her to resign. By this time she had 'really got her heels stuck in', so she refused that request, too, and the matter went to the local advisory committee which advises the Lord Chancellor's Department.

This is 'a very secret group of people which nobody knows about, and I wasn't allowed to go. I was allowed to write, but I didn't know what they were going to accuse me of so I didn't know what to defend myself with.' She stated her case, as she saw it, and it went to the Lord Chancellor's Department. The result was predictable: she was 'deemed to have brought the magistracy into disrepute and removed from the bench'.

The National Council for Civil Liberties (NCCL), which had taken an interest in her case, advised her that she could appeal against the Lord Chancellor's decision. Having been convinced that her civil rights were being misused, she was happy to follow their suggestion. The normal procedure is for a barrister to put the case to a judge who then decides whether or not to allow an appeal. However, in Kath's case, the Lord Chancellor's Department at the eleventh hour sent down a QC to put the other side.

As a result, not only was she refused leave to appeal, but the QC asked for costs to be given against her, which could have been around £3,000. They appealed against this immediately: 'It's justice for the rich, isn't it?' Her case could have been taken to the European Court, but they did not have the finance.

'It was very good from the point of view of all the people who knew me, because these issues were suddenly important to them, they didn't think that an ordinary citizen like Kath Cripps could have a D Notice slapped on her.' She had no definite proof of this, but a journalist friend told her that this was the case, because as soon as she appealed against the Lord Chancellor's decision all the press clamour stopped. This was a welcome respite, but she soon became aware of being the focus of attention from a different source.

One morning as I was going to work a police motor cyclist going in the other direction did a U-turn and came up behind me and followed me to the hospital. Then a friend of mine borrowed my car to go across town one lunchtime, and came back shaking. She'd picked up three separate police tails, so there was definitely something going on – but I preferred not to think about it.

Part of the explanation for the national media interest in her case was that she had set a precedent. No one had ever challenged the Lord Chancellor's decision on that issue before. At about the same time, the form filled in by potential magistrates was changed to include a question about membership of CND.

She was told that she was free to reapply to the bench, which she felt was ludicrous: 'The idea of sitting up there now, to me is horrendous . . . it's left me with no faith really in the judicial system.'

An NCCL study after her case showed that the bulk of magistrates come from the better-class areas and are not representative of the population as a whole. Although in her area there was a fair sprinkling of women who were Labour Party nominees, she says that they were not working people who knew what was happening at grass-roots level. As a result of her experience, she is convinced that the benches are very biased.

Is it better for the people standing in front of me on the bench to know that I'm a CND member or not to know? If they think that what I believe in is going to prejudice their case, they can say so. They can't say so if they don't know . . . You could be a member of the Rotary Club – or anything else – and that didn't matter. But to me it's no more prejudicial to be a member of CND than all these other things they were members of . . . They would say you could be a member of CND, but you're not allowed to be an active member.

So, why are some people, like Kath, active, and others not?

They just aren't aware of the problems, or they see them as unsurmountable. You run up against it all the time – 'there's nothing I can do'. They don't see that one person can do anything. I can remember sitting in a pub one night with this bloke, a member of the CND group, and he bought a Mars bar and a Kitkat bar, and he was talking in this vein about how our one little group in a really anti area couldn't do anything. And I started talking to him about these chocolate bars which were both from taboo firms at the time, which we were supposed to be boycotting. And he left the chocolate bars on the bar and didn't eat them. So, at the end of the evening, I said to him, 'So are you going to eat those chocolate bars then?', and he said 'No'. To me that was the power of one person – just me in that instance – talking to him. And when I said to him, do you realise I by myself have stopped you from eating those chocolate bars, then it sort of flattened the whole of his other argument. And this was a bloke who was a fairly active member . . . The problem really is apathy. People like their own little life the way they lead it and they don't want to get involved in anything else.

The only way she knows to encourage people to be active is to keep on talking to them about the issues. She thinks that CND's activities will continue at their present level until something happens some-where that will raise people's awareness of the dangers and lead to greater support than at present. 'One just hopes that it isn't anything too terrible that happens to do that.'

As a result of an Open Space TV programme she was asked to do after her case, Kath was invited to be an adviser on the programme's committee, which looks at submissions of new ideas.

There was a programme recently whose first half was on Sizewell B nuclear power station, which showed that in spite of the huge protest that the people there had made, it had been built, and people were saying that there's no democracy. It doesn't matter what we do, what we say, we just run into this huge wall of government, or whatever it happens to be. But the second half of the programme was about the new [power station] at Hinckley Point, and there they were saying that there is still hope, that we've got to fight this one, even though they lost that one. And they were managing to generate quite a lot of enthusiasm there. They were using things like Chernobyl that had happened since the Sizewell inquiry. And, in a way, it has to be something that actually affects the people themselves for them to get up and have some kind of enthusiasm . . . It's very difficult to get people to see things from other people's points of view. It's always, 'well, it won't happen, we'll put it to the back of our minds.'

Kath's anti-nuclear activities were once again to bring her into conflict with the law. In November 1986 she took part in a symbolic 'snowball' action of cutting one strand of wire at the British Nuclear Fuels Ltd (BNFL) plant at Capenhurst, Cheshire, which processes uranium. She was arrested and eventually taken to a cell in Chester police station. She decided to plead 'not guilty', on the grounds that she had been causing necessary damage to prevent a greater evil.

When she came before Bakewell court (where a former colleague sat on the bench) the following January, she was the only one of all the accused to be cross-examined. She eventually was found guilty and fined £100 and £45 costs. Kath paid the costs, so that she could not be accused of wasting tax-payers' money, but refused to pay the £100, expecting to go to prison. But instead, the court used an attachment of earnings order to take £20 a month of her wages to pay the fine.

Undeterred, Kath joined a CND protest at the US listening station at Menwith Hill on American Independence Day, 4 July 1987, to ask for British independence from US surveillance. As they walked round the public footpath on the perimeter of the base, they found that their every step was being followed by a camera from inside.

More recently, Kath has found a new area to engage her interest and energies. Since her decision to leave her marriage, her experience of living on her own has led her to believe that there is a need for a support group for women trapped in unhappy relationships. Achieving her independence, while remaining on good terms with her former husband, has left her elated, and she wants to help others to find the courage to do the same. Kath believes that dependency of women on their partners is a major problem of our society, and no doubt she will be as active in this issue, as she is in campaigning for peace.

CHAPTER 12

GORDON BAXENDALE AND IRIS WILLIAMS

I think if there was a change of government . . . We would still want tenant participation . . . Getting something done, and getting a proper result, that's the satisfaction, really.

Gordon Baxendale

Wrexham Maelor, like other parts of Wales, has been devastated by pit closures, and the loss of thousands of jobs at Shotton Steel Works was another heavy blow. Unemployment has forced many to live on benefit, there is a high incidence of one-parent families needing special support, and many people are reliant on council housing.

'They're not council houses, they're tenants' houses', is the view of Gordon Baxendale, the toughest fighter for tenants' rights in the area. Perched in a crow's nest of a tiny, smoky top-floor room in the offices of Shelter Wales, Gordon, who served in the Navy for 30 years and is now registered as disabled, believes an active citizen is just the same as a good citizen or a good neighbour. 'If you see areas where there is a general feeling within your own community that something wants doing, then you attempt to get something done about it.'

Gordon is vice-chairman of his tenants' association, and chairman of the Wrexham Borough Tenants Federation, a group of 16 tenants' associations that have got together to present one voice on major issues such as the Housing Acts. He is also on the Department of Social Security Consumer Committee which keeps a watch on the service the local DSS gives its clients, and hopes to influence national policies for the benefit of local people who use the service. He recently joined the steering committee of the Tenants Participation Advisory Service (TPAS Wales), launched in summer 1989 to help train people to keep tenants throughout Wales informed of their rights and the procedures for getting them.

It was local problems on his own housing estate that got him involved in this field. There were a number of difficulties with repairs, the general state of the communal areas was bad, and the play areas for the children were dangerous. So about six tenants decided to get together and do something about it. They formed their own tenants' association, working closely with Shelter Wales 'because they deal with homeless, and I am sure they would agree that a vast percentage of their actual homeless are ex-council tenants'.

Their association is funded mainly by contributions from tenants, 50 pence a year if they are unemployed or senior citizens, £1 if they are in full employment. Other tenants' associations do not take subscriptions, but raise money from bingo sessions and coffee mornings. Most get a donation from the Community Council. Shelter Wales gives a starter grant to all associations and the Welsh Community Agency also gives funding.

His tenants' association is always trying to get money out of the council, with whom it has developed a love-hate relationship. As a general rule, it works with the council, getting strong support from some officers, who agree that tenants should have a say in decision-making. Other officers and councillors, however, feel threatened by the association's interest in how the council's money is spent.

We know we are the consumers and we know it's our money, but they say why should we have a say, we haven't had one before? What are councillors there for – they're elected. But we are also elected, and if you look at some of the associations, we possibly have a much larger nomination in numerical strength than the council have at council elections. We are about 90 per cent representative of my given area because people say 'yes, we want an association, yes we want you to represent us, here's my 50 pence'. So we give them a receipt and say 'you've joined'.

But the support of the local community varies: 'It depends what's on television, whether it's raining, whether it's their night for bingo.' Their biggest hurdle is public apathy: 'If you have a major problem, such as a rat-infested river or major pollution, or they are going to build an inflow-filled tip – which they are trying to do in three areas around here – you can get everyone to the public meeting.' If, however, it is about something which involves a minority of the community, for example, old-age pensioners or children's playgroups, they do not always get a good turnout: 'So you can't say that with every issue you are fully representative, because everyone has different aspirations and needs.'

They have a rule that, unless it is an emergency they do not take up individual complaints. First, tenants have to go through the full council procedure, 'which can be quite nauseatingly long-winded'.

Gordon is very concerned about the effects of the community charge on the local community: 'I have not found one person who is for the poll tax . . . I think if the elderly were affected badly the community would react very, very strongly and they would be up in arms.' He is also afraid that it will exacerbate problems of homelessness amongst young people.

> If the kids don't get on too well with Mum and Dad, they're unemployed, and some officer who has the authority goes to the house and says you have got to pay the poll tax, it is a legal requirement, then shortly Mum and Dad are going to say to those kids, on your bike . . .

Why is Gordon so active and involved in his community, while others may only be interested in what goes on in their back gardens? Gordon believes his 'social conscience' must have grown while he was in the Navy, leaving a wife and children behind:

> You start thinking how is the missus going to manage, who is going to mend the fuse for her when it goes, all sorts of little things . . . Maybe you had to think more about your domestic circumstances, so that builds up in you and it becomes the normal thing to do, to make sure that next door or Mrs Bloggs is OK because her husband has gone to sea.

Also, he feels that 'a ship or a barracks is only a community, lots of people thrown together to live and work and you have got to do it. You don't have to do it in civilian life, so maybe it is self-discipline.' He likes to think that the area in which he lives is as pleasant as it can be, with the streets reasonably swept and clean: 'Maybe it is just a personal idea, but there must be hundreds and thousands like me.'

So how does he get community support? First, if there is a problem, he gets people together to discuss it, and to agree that they want to do something: 'If you can't get them to agree that a) there is a problem, or b) they want to solve it, you may as well almost give up. We don't, we keep battling on.' But he feels that active citizens like himself have to be careful not to become do-gooders, or to push their personal ideas: 'One of the criticisms levelled at you is the fact that you're doing it for yourself. Do you want your name in the paper? Do you want to be the leader of the community? All sorts, that's where you have got to be very careful.'

Another difficulty is trying to keep the impetus going once the initial problem has been solved. Sometimes people get bored with an activity like bingo. 'But hopefully then they will come up with another idea – couldn't we have so and so? – and that to me is the only way, though it's an awfully slow process.'

He believes that you must be political – though not party political.

I think if there was a change of government there would still be problems that we would have to surmount. We would still want tenant participation, we would still want our say . . . Getting something done, and getting a proper result, that's the satisfaction, really.

Iris Williams

Iris Williams' local tenants' association is a member of the Wrexham Borough Tenants Federation, of which Gordon is chairman. Mother of eight, grandmother of 13, 57-year-old Iris worked as a barmaid until, in early 1987, she chanced to go to a tenants' meeting one evening at her council estate at Llay, on the outskirts of Wrexham. That meeting changed her life: 'While I was there they got me to go on the committee, and within three months I was chairperson. Since then it has sort of snowballed.'

Iris is a natural carer. Now that most of her family have left home she has found replacements. There are tiny new arrivals in the tropical fish tank – 'my babies'. She is making a shawl for the baby of an 18-year-old who has been thrown out by her parents. And there are the tenants:

It's mostly people knocking at your door wanting advice, and I put them in touch with the right people. We just help people who come. We run a luncheon club held in the school canteen, we have about 30 to 35 old-age pensioners twice a week. We have a DSS officer here once a month for people to come and talk with him. I do other work besides with disabled people who need help.

Apart from the treasurer, Iris seems to run the tenants' association on her own. 'You don't get any help. I've tried for help but they just don't want to know. They've had their jobs done, had their houses done, their problems sorted out. So they don't want to know you any more.'

Outside help is, however, available from the Probation Office:

If I want jobs doing for old-age pensioners or disabled people I get in touch with the probation officer and they allow me to have two or three boys doing community service on a Saturday and Sunday to put up gates or fences or even a drive for someone, or decorating. There's a lady of 84, for instance, she's been doing her own all the time, but she finds she can't do it now. The council refused to just emulsion her stairs, they refused point blank. I tried everything to get them to do it, but no way. So I got the boys and they've done a wonderful job for her.

Relations with the council are crucial, and she feels that she could do a lot more if she was given more support.

I think we can do with somebody in the village like me who has plenty to say when they want to. The previous estate manager was wonderful, he worked with us really well. He'd meet with us once a month, he'd come to my house and phone me up if there was a problem. We'd help each other. This one just doesn't want to know. He thinks it's all a waste of time, association business. He's even put in a report saying there is no longer a tenants' association. The reason is because I won't go to see him. I know the sort of answers I'm going to get off him before I go, 'I can't tell you this, I can't tell you that.' I'm having the same problem with the councillors, they don't even look at me today, they seem to think I'm taking their job off them. But I'm not, I'm trying to help them with their work. They won't go round the village looking at what wants doing, so people come here instead.

As a result, Iris is on call 24 hours a day:

I had one woman here from Colwyn Bay one day on a Sunday with three children, homeless. It was 8 o'clock at night when I was having my lunch. She'd heard of me because they'd sent a leaflet all round the countryside and my name happened to be on it. I managed to get in touch with Shelter Wales in the end, by then it was late at night, and they took them. I get all sorts here. There was a woman who came and asked whether she should get married again. I said, if he's got money marry him, if he hasn't leave him.

She managed to get a grant from Opportunities for Volunteering in Wales to start a hire service for garden tools. But unfortunately, having hired them out for £1, she would get them back broken.

They're getting paid, you see. An old fellow used to borrow a lawn-mower, he would do six or seven lawns before he brought it back. Well, he was raking in about £16 to £20 a day, and I was only getting £1 for the lawn-mower. I don't blame him, he was clever. But it's abusing the system.

So what makes all the work worthwhile to her?

I think it's just the thought that I can help somebody. It's mostly the old-age pensioners that get to me – they're like children. They seem to come to me for everything. If they want a washer on the tap, send for Iris. If the iron is broken, it's send for Brian [her husband]. If somebody's locked out I have to go with a ladder and climb through bedroom windows. But I love the challenge of it, I like to be able to think I can do it.

How does Iris cope with the burden of other people's problems?

I don't let it worry me, once they've gone from the door. It's only their troubles and I've done something for them. Sometimes it will crop up in my mind and I'll think, poor devils, is there anything else I can do? But I force myself not to worry about them. That would crack you up. I'm that type of person, I can laugh at anything.

As well as Iris's sense of humour, bingo also helps to take her mind off things. But there are times, nevertheless, when she is sorely tested.

A woman had a burst pipe one night, 12.00 at night, pouring with rain. We had a phone call and I thought it was one of the children. A woman was screaming her head off at the other end, 'I'm flooded out, me carpets are six inches of water and it's going up the stairs.' So I got her name and address and I said, 'have you been for a councillor?' 'Oh no, we don't bother with them.' So we had to run like hell, going through all that rain. She was really in a mess, it was disgusting. I rushed back here and phoned the emergency services, and the fellow was too damn drunk to answer the phone, you should have heard him. So I rang for a councillor. 'Well, my garden is flooded', he said, and I said, 'this isn't a damn garden, it's a house, she is absolutely lumbered up with it, it's everywhere water.' Anyway, he came down an hour after, and he said, 'There's nothing I can do tonight.' I blew my top. I got back on to the emergency and managed to get a group of men to come and pump the water out, we were there to 3 o'clock in the morning. The councillor had gone back home – because his garden had been flooded. There are some days when I could feel like throwing things at people who knock at the door.

CHAPTER 13

ELAINE APPELBEE

*We have a community there now and people do respond to each
other's needs. That's citizenship – being part of another, being
part of the same body. Active citizenship is involvement with each
other, isn't it?*

The parish of Little Horton in inner-city Bradford is a place full of
contradictions. Dominated by the huge and imposing Victorian
church of All Saints, the upkeep of which its parishioners can barely
afford, the area is now home to a large Asian community. They live in
decaying properties which were once the homes of the wealthy textile
mill-owners who, having made their money near the centre of the city,
moved up the hillside to green fields and cleaner air.

Nor has the parish escaped the depredations of the twentieth
century. Around 300 mostly white families, many of them single-
parent households, live in two dozen grim, low-rise maisonettes in
Hutson Street. Their problems, and those of everyone living in the
parish, are also very much of this century. Twenty-three per cent of
people in the area are unemployed – in some parts, like the
Canterbury estate, it reaches 86 per cent; 40 per cent are semi-skilled,
which in Bradford means low wages. Eighteen per cent are elderly
and 12 per cent are under five.

'All this', says Elaine Appelbee, who works for the Mothers' Union
at the Hutson Street project, 'means that we have a population here
that is 100 per cent economically vulnerable.' The maisonettes tend to
be the first rung on the housing ladder for their tenants. If they stay a
year and are judged to be good tenants, they may be lucky enough to
be offered a better property in a different part of the town.

Elaine Appelbee, now 35, is a committed Christian. In addition to
her paid employment at the Hutson Street project, she is also very
active in other areas of Church work. She is a member of
Communities, Churches and Charities Alliance, a local group

working around the issue of poverty. Last year they organised a conference on the issue in Bradford.

She is also a member of the Bishop's Council – in effect, a group of advisers to the Bishop of Bradford – as well as having a family of her own.

Although she works with two social workers from the council, her work at the Hutson Street project is funded by the Church of England's Urban Fund. The project is the only community resource in the area. The parade of shops which once graced the estate is now boarded up, apart from one grocery store.

'When we first started working here nearly two years ago we were looking for an area that was not having any of its needs met', says Elaine. 'We now have this little shop – the meeting room is 18 feet square – and that's what we've made into a community centre.' She and her colleagues had to go out and knock on people's doors to get them to come and meet each other.

What we've done is brought people together. And instead of saying to them – what you need is this or that, we've worked very much from listening, picking up on their ideas and supporting them in putting their ideas into practice. We encouraged them to see that if they come together, they can actually affect the quality of their life.

At the project there is now a parent and under-fives group, an active tenants' association and a friendship group for older people, or those whose children have gone to school. There is also a literacy and return to learn group.

Once they gain confidence they want to move on. There is a tremendous potential in people which is really exciting. They can come to this class and do the return to learn course. We've already had one woman who has trained to be a playgroup leader and has gone on to do her NNEB [childcare qualification] at college. The whole focus of the project – as I'm working from a Church base – is that every hair on people's heads will be counted. We're trying to counter the very strong message that comes through the media that, if you're unemployed or a single parent, then you are failing, you're worthless, you've got nothing to offer anybody.

Elaine is conscious of the fact that she is, to some extent, an outsider. Is there a danger that everything which happens in Hutson Street is dependent on her and her colleagues and that, when they withdraw, there will be no momentum to carry things forward? She recognises that it is unrealistic to say that people in the community do not depend on her to some degree, but confidence is growing. The playgroup – a small group, but in the context of the area a major achievement – already virtually runs itself.

> We have a meeting every three weeks to support people and they can come to us as a backstop – but otherwise they run things. Our aim is to have a users' group and eventually to feed people through onto the management. What we're trying to do is be sensitive to people's development and, when they are ready, for them to say it, not for us to make a judgement about it. In the end, what's going to change life for people in the inner cities is themselves believing that . . . they really count so that they won't stand being treated badly. That's the next breakthrough that's got to happen in our work if we're going to move beyond charity.

Although her co-workers are not practising Christians, Elaine says that they bring many of the same qualities to their work: 'They just don't acknowledge it in the way that I would see it', she says. As for her own beliefs and how they relate to working in a deprived inner-city area, not directly pushing her faith or making her work in any way conditional on their attitude to her religion, she is remarkably direct:

> There would be Christians who would say it is part of our belief that we have to serve people, but I think it's much stronger than that. In the Bible there is a very clear message – God likes to turn things upside down. And the message is that the rich will only find their healing or salvation if they are absolutely focused down and working with people who are suffering – and not only in the sense of charity, but going beyond that into justice, the deal being that none of us has a claim on God's love, no right to it. The deal is you pass it on to people who have no claim on you. I think we've lost that focus in the Church and it's one reason why the Church is dying on its feet.

Elaine's religious beliefs inform the way she helps to run the groups which meet at the Hutson Street project. And she feels that we are judged by our attitude to society and, in particular, to the losers.

So how do we treat those losers? Our salvation will depend on how we, as a community, treat the losers. That is the one thing the Church has lost. The sense that we are not expected to live out the Gospel on our own, but that we are supposed to work, wherever we are, together. These are the kinds of things, in a tiny way, that we are trying to do at Hutson Street. It's more than just getting people into the Church buildings.

'God doesn't see worship as just praying on a Sunday. In fact, He said none of that works unless your worship is also working in obedience to what He wants – focusing on those who are losing out.'

But surely that means that the gathering together and empowering of a community is dependent on an acknowledged Christian belief? Elaine does not think this is so. The Church has to ally with people and God may be working through them, even if they do not accept His existence. Hutson Street is important precisely because it shows that the Church is willing to work with other people. It is, according to Elaine, a new tradition, or rather a rediscovered tradition.

She admits that when she first began to understand what she now calls a kind of liberation theology, many of her fellow Christians would not accept her views. 'It sent me home in tears from one or two meetings', she says. Then, through her interest in Liberation theology and the Base Christian communities in South America, she began to find out that there were other people who thought like her.

Not only did they think like that, but they were acting on that and it was making a real difference. They were still able to do it within the context of the institutional Church, but they weren't banging their heads against it trying to change it. They were just acting in obedience to God on their little patch. Be obedient where you are and things will happen. And they certainly have. What it comes down to is a synthesis between good community work practice and faith. And we are trying, in a very clumsy way, to work that out in a British situation as opposed to a Latin American one.

Elaine is aware that her views are not always popular within the Church. 'I've had comments that I'm a party political broadcast for the Labour Party, for example, or "the other side".' But she argues that the basis of everything she says and does is in the Gospel. When she explains where her views come from, even traditionally conservative groups like the Mothers' Union find they can support her: 'I speak to a lot of Mothers' Union groups and yet they have no trouble with what I have to say. They get excited and enthused and I think that Faith comes alive.'

Elaine says that the traditional Church has somehow managed to rationalise all the powerful, stimulating, unnerving and frightening aspects of belief out of itself and, in doing so, has become tedious and lacking in meaning to many people.

We have to say to those comfortable Christians, 'without you playing your part, both as Christians and within society, nothing is going to change'. And I see myself, in a tiny way, as trying to help that happen. The basis of it all is the issue of justice – that we've got people living in this country in a way that is unacceptable.

And what does that mean in terms of citizenship? She thinks that, for many people, it probably means nothing, because they do not actually feel that they are citizens. They have no status or confidence. They have been actively damaged by society. They have no stake in it and are beaten by it.

I suppose it's really around the idea of the Fourth World – the excluded, the people who don't count. And I'm sure the excluded of the First World and the Third World would recognise each other quite easily. In one of the community groups we were talking about the effects of the Social Security Act and the local council cutbacks and one woman said, 'Well, under each blow you just bend'. But, at some point, you break. What amazes me is just how courageous people are.

But there is a price to be paid. Elaine points to the tremendous loss of potential to the community.

There is so much people can do and would want to do, given the chance to participate. But that doesn't seem to be in society's interests to suddenly have this extra fifth of the population suddenly asking awkward questions, in fact being active citizens. Because that implies they can make decisions politically. People say they've got the vote, but that means nothing. They feel disenfranchised. They don't even begin to think that anybody would listen, and that's the starting point. Because we are the first people that have listened.

But simply getting people to become more confident and conscious of their own capabilities is not the objective of Elaine's Christian aspirations. It is important to go on from there to actively work for justice for people who are excluded. 'This is where I get accused of being idealistic', she says, 'but if you pass on the love that you get, it automatically makes for a just society. As a Christian, that is what I mean by building the Kingdom of God.'

While we continue to think of the Church as the buildings we have got, that people can only discover God if they come into those buildings on our terms, that is limiting and narrowing God's vision. It's killing the Church. The Gospel is about change, movement and risk-taking.

It has become clear that there is a close connection between what Elaine regards as an active form of Christianity and active citizenship.

When you see people come together, it is not dull. They have better scripts than *Neighbours*! When they get to know each other, they begin to care. And if you care you will respond. That's the stage we are at with the project in Hutson Street. We have a community there now and people *do* respond to each other's needs. That's citizenship – being part of another, being part of the same body. Active citizenship is involvement with each other, isn't it?

CHAPTER 14

PROFILE OF A VOLUNTARY WORKER

These are people who are not satisfied with the world as it is . . .
They have a vision and what keeps them going is their hope that
they can achieve it.

It is immediately obvious from reading about the individuals in the preceding pages that you cannot tell who are volunteers by the look of them. Voluntary workers evidently come in all shapes and sizes, all ages and sexes, every race and religion and culture. Some are paid for what they do; others relish their freedom to go their own way. They were obviously not chosen to appear in this book because they are exceptional in some way. I know they would agree with me that they are essentially ordinary people; indeed, it is precisely for that reason that their experiences are reported here.

Looking at what they do is equally unhelpful in arriving at a conclusion as to what goes to make up a voluntary worker. There is one of this and two of that, but no apparent common pattern. It seems as if the form the object of their activity takes is irrelevant. It can range from conservation to getting drains unblocked, from bringing the arts to people starved of culture to serving in the tea bar at an out-patients' clinic. There are as many 'causes' as there are volunteers to support them, and each of the people interviewed is involved in some quite different activity. What is common to them all is clearly not the target they aim at, but some other more elusive quality.

What is it that impels them to devote so much time and energy to something for which there may be little tangible reward and often considerable cost? Why ever do they bother? Here again the mixture is as before. This is an identity parade where everyone is different. With some, it is a moral imperative; with others, inspiration comes from a political ideal. With others again, there is the contentment that comes from finding something worth doing in an otherwise

unremarkable life. Unkind critics might perhaps label them as
busybodies, or accuse them of being dogmatists out to conduct some
personal mission to those they regard as benighted. No doubt they are
often disparagingly termed 'do-gooders'. They themselves spend
little time considering whether they can be classed as active citizens or
voluntary workers.

The Common Bond of Self-fulfilment

Yet what is quite remarkable is that out of what, at first sight, might
seem to be a random collection of individual experiences and
opinions, a surprising uniformity in fact emerges. These are birds of a
feather, however different their plumage might appear to be. A sense
of unity underlies their apparently diverse activities. What is more,
they are obviously direct inheritors of the tradition of all those who
throughout the century have clung to their determination to make a
personal contribution to the affairs of the community of which they
are members.

What is that common bond? It may seem paradoxical to suggest
that the starting point in trying to track down this elusive quality lies
in the fact of the immense satisfaction they derive from their
activities. It is shiningly evident that the giving of service brings with
it an extraordinary feeling of happiness, though the word seems
wildly incongruous in regard to people whose labours are so often
directed to the relief of great unhappiness in others. They might
almost be said to be having fun, except that there can be nothing
funny about being wakened in the middle of the night to go to the
rescue of some neighbour whose home has been flooded. I remember
that my husband used to say that I ought to pay to be allowed to be a
Councillor because of the immense pleasure I derived from the job.

To interpret this as proof positive of the self-seeking motives of a
bunch of 'do-gooders' would be a gross misinterpretation. It is,
nevertheless, a pointer of immense significance. Reading between the
lines of these interviews, it is evident that it is the relationship with
others, the feeling of belonging to whatever community they find
themselves in, that matters every bit as much as, if not more than, any
particular objective. It was through being of service to others that the
people described above found themselves. One contributor specifically talks of her commitment to her particular pursuit as having
brought her a sense of liberation. Others, less vocal, nevertheless
radiate the same deep sense of fulfilment. The lesson to be learned

from people such as these is that what Richard Titmuss called 'the gift relationship' (*The Gift Relationship*, 1970) is a factor in our lives which we, as a society, neglect at our peril. The welfare state is designed to ensure our survival as individuals, but pays little heed to our universal need to be of value to the society we live in.

The Vision of a Better World

Quite unexpectedly, this makes it clear that there is, in fact, a distinction to be drawn as between the voluntary worker and the active citizen. What these people do owes its origin to some quite other motive than that of the duty of a citizen to the state, upright and law-abiding though they undoubtedly are. Academics talk of this personal inspiration as stemming from the 'value base' by which each of us determines our daily course through life. Some will prefer to call it 'conscience' or an 'inner light'. Regardless of the label, what matters is most emphatically not something imposed on them from without, but arises from a strictly personal reaction to the world about them. You do not stand protesting outside the very court where you yourself sit as a magistrate, as did Kath Cripps, out of loyalty to those who appointed you. Nor is it for that reason that Gordon Baxendale and Iris Williams slog around housing estates demanding fair play for tenants to the exasperation of the establishment. Nor undertake any of the multitude of activities pursued by the thousands of others throughout our society who voluntarily give service.

What is this gift that they have to give? The answer is so old-fashioned as to be barely credible in this day and age, yet there is no other word for it. Their purpose is nothing other than betterment. One or two actually use the word, but it is implicit in every interview. These are people who are not satisfied with the world as it is. They have other ideas as to what life could be or ought to be about. They have a vision and what keeps them going is their hope that they can achieve it. They live in faith.

What constitutes that blessed state of betterment is irrelevant. Maybe it is nothing more ambitious than that we should be more caring towards each other, more willing to take on the small kindnesses of a good neighbour. Maybe it is nothing less than headline-hitting stuff which a century ago would have earned them the label of dissenters. It was no coincidence that the impressive lead given to the movement for social reform in Liverpool came largely from Nonconformists.

What matters is that, however large or small the target of their intention, they are not prepared to sit back and leave it to others to 'do something' about it. Confronted by the faceless bureaucracy of the welfare state, they stubbornly present their human face. It is this active commitment to their belief that the world could be a better place that is the gift they have to offer. It is a gift of priceless value because, without a vision, the people perish.

A Word of Warning

One last word of warning. Judging by these reports voluntary service is obviously not a matter of roses, roses all the way. Liberation, self-fulfilment, dedication to some cause great or small, may bring infinite satisfaction, but there is a price to be paid which can be high. Disillusion, heartbreak, frustration in the face of injustice and indifference, physical and moral fatigue – all these may have to be endured. More than one marriage has suffered as a consequence of the assertion of freedom which voluntary service brings with it, especially on the part of women. The pure theory of volunteering is easily confused by its entanglement with the dilemma of women today which sets them free to move in the world outside the family without releasing them from the bonds of domestic tradition. We have a long way to go before we can talk of volunteering as a universal experience, freely available to all.

These are problems for the future. What light does all this throw on the part to be played by the voluntary movement in the changing world into which we are now entering? The issue is one of fundamental importance to the future of the democratic society to which we belong, and the final chapter of this book is therefore devoted to looking at the way ahead.

PART THREE

THE FUTURE

Margaret Simey

CHAPTER 15

THE WAY AHEAD

It is essential for the survival of our way of life that the right to love our neighbours, freely and without compulsion, wins recognition as the true basis of all citizenship.

Where do we go from here? One thing is certain. There can be no going back to the customs and practices of the charitable in the past. For good or ill, all that is over and done with. My immediate reaction when I first read about the voluntary workers portrayed above was to cry out in astonishment – how times have changed! The very fact that these individuals were chosen because they represent the wide spread of voluntary work today is evidence of the change that has come over the scene. Remembering the earnest little bunch of women who were students at the School of Social Science in my day, the contrast could not be more dramatic. The nature of the 'pool' available for the giving of voluntary service has altered beyond belief.

Equally striking is the extent to which our ideas have changed as to the nature of voluntary work and what part, if any, it has to play in the world of the welfare state. There seems to be little scope and less enthusiasm for personal service in the centralised government of today. The change is dramatically illustrated by the contrast between the determination with which women like Dorothy Keeling defended their territory against takeover by the state (see page 6), and the acquiescence with which Manpower Services projects in recent years tolerated their dependence on government control.

As for active citizenship, such talk has not been heard since my days as a cadet in the suffragist movement. Then, women were preparing themselves for the exercise of the right as citizens to vote which they hoped would shortly be theirs. This must obviously be up-dated. Universal suffrage has been won, but the right to vote is no longer regarded as the key to social responsibility. A whole new job specification covering the rights and duties of the citizen is urgently required if the plea for a more active citizenship is to succeed.

And just at this very moment, when the decline in the numbers of voluntary workers is a cause of anxious concern to many of us, the situation has taken a totally unexpected turn. As a matter of policy, responsibility on a vast scale is being shifted from locally elected representatives and the official bureaucracy directly to voluntary agencies. On occasion, participation by the consumers, as they are now called, is actually built in to the legislation, as in the case of school government. At first sight, this might seem to be a triumph for the voluntary principle but, in reality, the outcome is deeply disturbing. Housing associations, for example, indignantly assert their autonomy as voluntary bodies, but their scope for independent decision is constantly under threat by reason of their dependence on central government funding. Simultaneously, the sheer magnitude of the extended responsibilities now pressed upon them means that they are forced to rely increasingly on the services of highly-paid professional executives. Many of these loyally strive to maintain the reality of control by their voluntary committee members, but find it increasingly difficult to do so.

The story could be duplicated right across the board in the voluntary sector. The experience of the voluntary bodies who became involved with Manpower Services schemes or are currently engaged in the whole range of services called community care, provoke many to fresh thought. How 'voluntary' are agencies which are heavily dependent on government support and administered by professional executives? How much scope is there for the pursuit of their original charitable intention when their performance is subjected to official monitoring in terms of their value for money?

Citizenship and Voluntary Service

Floundering in this sea of change and consequent uncertainty, the distinction between citizenship and voluntary service has become blurred in practice almost to the point of obliteration. Hence the loss of confidence and sense of direction which currently afflicts the voluntary movement. The present sorry state of the youth service is only one instance amongst many which illustrates the widespread failure to grasp the true significance of voluntaryism as distinct from citizenship.

It is, however, easier to spell out that difference in words than it is to put it into practice. In theory, citizenship is the label we give to the contract which governs the relationship between the state and ourselves as individuals. As citizens, every one of us is entitled to claim whatever privileges spring from being a member of what is called the body politic and, in return, we are required to undertake certain duties. It is these constitutional duties that the active citizen is very properly urged to carry out with greater zeal. There is no question here of choice; there can be no opting out.

If citizenship can be said to be concerned with the relationship between government and governed, then voluntary work is clearly something quite different, and this was the conclusion which rather unexpectedly emerged from this book. The giving of service is a strictly personal matter which has to do with the way in which each of us relates to our fellow human beings. There can be no volunteering by a castaway on a desert island. It is only by working out a satisfying relationship with other people that we achieve anything like self-fulfilment. Obviously, this is nothing to do with the state. People cannot be compelled to volunteer. You can be made to pay your poll tax by order, but no one can compel you to love – or hate – your neighbour.

So far, so good. However, to render unto Caesar whichever of these dual obligations seems appropriate, which would seem to be the sensible thing to do, is by no means an easy maxim to put into practice. The trouble is that the two often appear to be one and the same thing. To be an active citizen surely implies a willingness to be of service to others, while to be engaged in voluntary work equally surely proves that you are a good citizen. What adds to the confusion is the fact that in this country we have no formal Bill of Rights, which sets out our constitutional rights and duties. This is the deficiency which Charter 88 is designed to make good. There is similarly no consensus as to our moral obligations towards our fellow human beings, such as that we experienced during the blitz in the Second World War. With the decline in church-going, it is largely left to each of us to steer our way through life as best we can in the light of whatever experience has taught us to be the truth.

Government and the Voluntary Sector

This is, of course, no new dilemma and it is for that reason that it was thought important to begin this book with a short history of what has happened during the past century. Throughout that time, the debate has been about the extent to which the state should take over responsibility for what had previously been left to voluntary action. In recent years, however, this division of labour has been replaced by the government's infiltration into the very heartland of the voluntary movement. The system of financial assistance has, to all intents and purposes, become an instrument of social control under which the role of the voluntary bodies has changed from that of giving service according to their choice to one where they are, in effect, agents of the government. This is a process which is supported by the increasing influence exerted by some, at least, of the grant-giving trusts. The outcome is the emergence of the professional executive as the leading figure in the negotiations between government and voluntary bodies.

The dilemma for voluntary organisations has become acute. Even those who take their place within the structure of government – such as the WRVS or St John Ambulance – are finding it increasingly difficult to accommodate the pressures brought to bear on them.

Given such a quandary, what guidance is to be derived from either past history or the evidence of the assortment of volunteers whose experiences are here presented to us? First, that though there is most certainly a difference between the two sets of obligations, it is most emphatically not a case of either/or. To be active as a citizen does not necessarily exclude an assertion of the individual right to give service. To be a volunteer does not necessarily mean that you evade your duties as a citizen, or that your activities constitute a threat to the government. Each is vital to the other. Citizenship and voluntary service are, in fact, complementary and mutually dependent. There must be the framework of an orderly and stable society in which the social and political rights of the individual are safeguarded, if the freedom to seek self-fulfilment is to be viable. At the same time, it is of paramount importance to any democratic government that the right of the individual to make a personal contribution to the general well-being should be protected. This is an absolute requirement in a free society. The extent to which volunteering flourishes is perhaps the best measure of the effectiveness of a democratic system.

The second lesson follows automatically. Since these are dual obligations, neither of which can be denied, the resolution of the apparent contradiction between them must surely lie in striking a balance between them. That being so, there can be no once-and-for-all solution. Maintaining a balance is essentially an on-going process as anyone who rides a bicycle well knows. The way forward lies in a constant endeavour to achieve that balance rather than in futile conflict or the lop-sided development of either at the expense of the other.

The endless complaints of helplessness and frustration which are universal these days, and the endless resentment of the controls exerted by Them over Us, are evidence enough that this balance is certainly not being achieved. There seems to be no room for ordinary people in the management of our common affairs, either as volunteers or as citizens. In all my experience, I have never known what is called the 'threshold of awareness' of our role as members of a human society to be so low. The implications of membership of the community in which we have our being are to many a closed book. The consequences are evident all about us. They are reflected in the shocking contrast between the squalor of our public lives compared with the affluence enjoyed by increasing numbers of individuals. It is vital to our survival as a democratic society that this imbalance should be corrected.

Citizenship and the Gift Relationship

Starting with the obligations of citizenship, no one would deny the urgency of the need for people today to take their civic responsibilities far more seriously. In a democracy, vast areas of public behaviour depend on the self-discipline of ordinary people. The breakdown of law and order, which is rightly a cause for widespread concern, stems from the erosion of active support for the common code of what is acceptable behaviour. The effect of the trend to central government, common to all political parties but greatly intensified in the past decade, has been to make people feel that the management of our public life is nothing to do with them. Citizenship is thought of in terms of rights and benefits, with scant attention being paid to the duties which are necessarily part of the political 'contract'.

The suffragists recognised the dangers of precisely such a development when they stressed the importance of educating women as to their rights and responsibilities, if and when they achieved the vote. Beveridge actually prophesied in the third volume of his great trilogy (*Voluntary Action. A Report on Methods of Social Advance*, 1948) that unless people accepted their obligations as citizens, all his proposals for setting them free from the five terrible giants of deprivation must surely fail. Significantly, it is a book to which reference is seldom made.

In contrast, the lack of enthusiasm for the voluntary giving of service is less visibly obvious. If large numbers decide to opt out of their civic duties and take to disorder on the streets and burglary in the night, the public are quickly aware of the consequences. But any ebbing away of support for the voluntary movement is hard to detect. Fewer volunteers behind the counters of the citizens advice bureaux or willing to do the donkey work of attending committee meetings makes little impact. The practical consequences are rightly a matter of great concern to many voluntary bodies.

Even more disturbing is the lack of comprehension of the fundamental importance of the 'gift relationship' as being essential to the democratic way of life. The basic importance of making sure that the individual shall survive is taken for granted; this, after all, is what the welfare state is all about. On the other hand, the fact that the need to belong to some human group in a meaningful way is equally essential to individual well-being is ignored. It is something that is assumed to be an irrelevance to life in the mass conurbations in which our lives are now set. The sad story of the neglect of the community development movement illustrates the point, as does the widespread inability to get to grips with the gang mentality which characterises the hooliganism associated with football and, most frighteningly, with the political groups committed to violence.

What of the Future?

What of the future? The familiar cry on every side is that it is always the same little handful who do all the work. The public at large seem to have abandoned all thought of social responsibility. Individualism rules OK. Yet, at the same time, what are we to make of the astonishing response to the TV appeals on behalf of charity? Write it off as a sentimental reaction to clever publicity if you will but, at the very least, it surely suggests that the capacity to care does still exist if only it can be tapped. As for the right to dissent, never in my long experience have I known anything like it. Protest groups spring up like mushrooms all over the place. A most unexpected by-product of the introduction of the poll tax is the heightened sense of community which it has roused in people who never before thought of marching the streets in step with a crowd of total strangers. We can all quote innumerable examples of this kind.

How can we turn this spontaneous reaction into a way of life that is squarely based on the principle of universal social responsibility? I believe that it is not apathy that defeats us but atrophy. Where there is no outlet for energy, it runs into the sands. The opportunity for either active citizenship or voluntary work has diminished beyond all recognition since my own early days as a social worker. The universal deprivation from which every one of us suffers in the modern world is that of the denial of access to social responsibility. We have been conditioned to dependence. In terms of active participation in a vital human society our lives are deeply impoverished. The experience of the sense of self-fulfilment which emerges so strikingly from the interviews in this book is all too rare an occurrence in the consumer society.

In part, this has come about because of the erosion of the tradition of service to others by the individualism which has characterised the eighties. The churches have a leading role to play in combatting this, as they are increasingly aware. But only in part. The voluntary movement must waken up to the fact that we pass the buck when we talk of the apathy of others. The fault is ours. We have created a welfare state, but we have ignored the far more pressing necessity to ensure the existence of the caring and just community of a welfare society.

Altruism grows by what it feeds on. Our strategy must be one of learning by doing. The appetite for service must be whetted by first-hand experience. A major re-think of what is defined as 'voluntary' is called for, so that it comprises a whole new range of activity in addition to the traditional expression of compassion for those in need. This raises the issue of political intervention, not least on the part of the churches. Yet the political activities of some voluntary organisations are surely evidence of that very independence of conscience which is the characteristic of the volunteer.

Imagination will be required and a willingness to face drastic change. We must abandon the trappings of Bumbledom with its automatic resort to committees as the only known form of democracy. The centralisation which is necessary to the conurbation society must be counter-balanced by a demand for the return of responsibility to grass-root levels in both voluntary and statutory agencies. The large voluntary organisations with their professional executives must grasp every opportunity to put their principles into practice.

Hope for the future lies in the fact that the swing of the pendulum is apparent which suggests that the nineties may see a new awareness that the urge to give service springs from some deep well of feeling which is not the preserve of a few, but is common to everyone. To be a voluntary worker used to be a perk of the middle classes. The growing support for the 'empowerment of the people', and such developments as the growth of the housing co-operative movement, are indications that the time has come for that privilege to become a universal right and a matter of common daily experience. The voluntary acceptance of personal responsibility for the well-being of others is the hall-mark of a democracy. It is essential for the survival of our way of life that the right to love our neighbours, freely and without compulsion, wins recognition as the true basis of all citizenship.

Index of Names

Other titles in the **Society Today** series:

Chris Heginbotham
Return to Community: The Voluntary Ethic and Community Care

Peter Newell
Children Are People Too: The Case Against Physical Punishment

Walter Schwarz
The New Dissenters: The Nonconformist Conscience in the Age of Thatcher

Margaret Simey
Government by Consent: The Principles and Practice of Accountability in Local Government

Colin Ward
The Child in the City

Colin Ward
The Child in the Country

Colin Ward
Welcome, Thinner City: Urban Survival in the 1990s

John Withington
Shutdown: The Anatomy of a Shipyard Closure

For further details, please write to the sales manager, Bedford Square Press, 26 Bedford Square, London WC1B 3HU